BUSINESS THAT MAKE REAL MONEY

Create Your Wealth Immediately
And For Your Future

Henry Stanley

Copyright © 2019

All rights reserved

All rights to this book are reserved. No permission is given for any part of this book to be reproduced, transmitted in any form or means; electronic or mechanical, stored in a retrieval system, photocopied, recorded, scanned, or otherwise. Any of these actions require the proper written permission of the publisher.

INTRODUCTION	5
CHAPTER ONE	8
INTRODUCING THE TECHNOLOGY DEVICE	8
CHAPTER TWO	23
KNOWING MORE ABOUT THE TECHNOLOGY DEVICE 1	23
CHAPTER THREE	52
THE LIMITATIONS	52
TYPES OF THE TECHNOLOGY DEVICE	55
CHAPTER FOUR	78
INDUSTRIAL USE OF THE TECHNOLOGY DEVICE	78
CHAPTER FIVE	104
MATERIALS AND OTHER COMPONENTS	104
CHAPTER SIX	112
STARTING A BUSINESS WITH TECHNOLOGY	112
CHAPTER SEVEN	129
MAKING YOUR BUSINESS KNOWN	129

CHAPTER EIGHT	141
WHAT TO HAVE FOR THE BUSINESS	141
CHAPTER NINE	149
DEALING WITH GENERAL BUSINESS CHALLENGES	149
CHAPTER TEN	164
KNOW SOME COMMON PRODUCTS OF THE DEVICE	164
CONCLUSION	172

Disclaimer

All knowledge contained in this book is given for informational and educational purposes only. The author is not in any way accountable for any results or outcomes that emanate from using this material. Constructive attempts have been made to provide information that is both accurate and effective, but the author is not bound for the accuracy or use/misuse of this information.

INTRODUCTION

This book *Business that makes real money: create your wealth immediately and for your future* is a sequel to my prior publication *How to make money: winning way now*. Just like the later, this book is geared toward giving every reader an insight into how best to utilize the result of technological advancement in our world to make money and live a fulfilled lifestyle that each reader has dreamed. There is wide use of different technological devices among industries, and individuals, which has brought about a big market worth billions of dollars. This has created a ready-market for everyone who wishes to make money and be part of the billions of US dollars that the market has to offer.

We are in the century where knowledge is key; hence, you need to give yourself to knowing so as to stay ahead in your games. In this book, you will know more about certain technological advancements, have an understanding 'about the specific industries that are ever in need of the new device technology is birthing from time to time, the way it works, and the different forms of the device. Also, you will learn the steps you need to take to start a business using one of the devices of technology in our present world, the tips on how to make the business grow, and make more profits than an average business person.

Finally, you will learn about the specific challenges that come with engaging in business using the technological device, and business generally, and the way to deal with each of those challenges. The aim of this book is to guide you into becoming successful by utilizing the technology in your reach. You need to be ready to learn and practice what this book has to offer. I hope to see your smiling face at the end of this book for a new horizon of knowledge you would have covered.

CHAPTER ONE

INTRODUCING THE TECHNOLOGY DEVICE

Technology has never receded, rather it evolves and birth newer devices that are used to make our daily experience more interesting. One of the devices that have evolved through the continual development of technology is the 3D printer and its technology. With its introduction, the process of manufacturing has been made easier, and professionals, engineers, and designers can now have access to their ideas in a tangible form in a matter of time faster than it was with the traditional technique. 3D printing has come to stay with the postulation of its marketing, reaching over US$20 billion in the year 2020. This is to show you the prospect this technological device has to offer. Hence, the need for my interest in this book.

3D printing involves the process of creating a three-dimensional object through the use of a digital file. The digital file is a computer-aided design model (CAD). 3D printing is often referred to as *Additive manufacturing*. The term *additive manufacturing* is often used because 3D printing involves the addition of materials in layers. The additive process has to do with the creation of an object through the laying down of successive layers of materials until the object is finally formed. The layers can be considered as a thin cross-section of the new object in a sliced horizontal form.

3D printing contrasts with the traditional method of printing that involves casting, forging, and machining processes. It is a subtractive form of manufacturing, and it involves the cutting out or hollowing out of a metal or plastic piece using a milling machine. With 3D printing, you can create complex shapes with the use of fewer materials, unlike the conventional method of manufacturing that requires more materials.

3D printing deals with many processes that bring together various materials or solidify the materials through the control of the computer in order to arrive at a three-dimensional object. Some of the materials added together include molecules, powder grains, etc. 3D has moved from height to height as the year runs by. It is no longer what it was in the 1990s when it was only considered perfect for the production of aesthetic prototypes or those that are functional. Then, it was considered *rapid prototyping*. However, when we talk about 3D printing in 2019, we are simply referring to a manufacturing process that is viable or suitable as an industrial-production technology. This level of improvement in 3D printing status is a result of the increase in the range of its precision, repeatability, and material. The original meaning 3D printing denotes a process of depositing binder materials on a powder bed with the use of inkjet printer heads layer by layer. Nonetheless, in recent times, the term has covered a wider meaning of additive-manufacturing techniques, including electron-beam additive manufacturing and selective laser melting.

HISTORICAL BACKGROUND OF 3D PRINTING

When we talk about the revolutionary technologies of the 21st century, 3D printing is a crucial part. It is the result of the technological advancement that makes it possible for everyone, including engineers, doctors, DIY enthusiasts, etc. to transform their ideas (in virtual form) to a tangible object that they can see and touch. 3D printing is not an overnight wonder; neither is it a yearlong achievement. It is a result of many years of painstaking collation of different technological ideas and passion for building a world of reality from the virtual one created in the minds of people. The development and history of 3D printing span across decades, and it will be discussed based on three stages, which are the *infancy stage, the Adolescent age, and the Maturity or Prime age.* The technology has been around with us since 40 years ago, and it has been making a wave. Before the three known stages of 3D development, there was a short-lived history behind its growth. Although it came into existence in the 20th century, however, its history can as well be traced to the 19th century. Some of the ideas that led to its formation erupted from 1800. A French *photo sculptor*, Francois Willem, in 1859, was noted for demonstrating the first 3D scanning technology in the world. He did his demonstration by using 24 cameras to capture his subjects from various distinct angles simultaneously. Also, there is a further step in its creation in the same century when Joseph E. Blather, an inventor, got awarded a patent for devising a method of creating 3D topographical maps through the use of the layering method, which is similar to what we have in 3D printing today. These two events were pointers to the later development of the present-day 3D printing, which came up over eight decades after the two events.

The Infancy Stage

The infancy stage of 3D printing began in 1981 when Hideo Kodama, who worked in the Nagoya Municipal Industrial Research Institute released an account based on a prototyping system. The prototyping system was a rapid functional one that uses photopolymers. The prototype system contained a solid printed model that was built in layers, with each layer corresponding to a cross-sectional slice in the model. From this development, a new stride was reached three years later in 1984, when Charles Hull made a new history in the development of 3D printing by inventing *Stereolithography*. Stereolithography paved the way for designers to create 3D models via digital data, which they end up using to create tangible objects.

A photopolymer is the essential element of stereolithography. The photopolymer is an acrylic-based material. The photopolymer will have to come in contact with a UV laser beam, thereby making the part that has direct contact with the sun to become a solid plastic in order to make the specific model the designer wants. With this new invention, many inventors were glad. Their joy stems from the fact that it is possible for them to test and prototype their designs with no huge amount of investment as upfront to manufacture.

Charles Hull's company move of creating the first stereolithographic apparatus machine in 1992 made it a reality to have complex parts fabricated in layers in a shorter period of time. Another important invention that year was the Selective Laser Sintering machine (SLS) produced by a startup – DTM. The SLS shoots a laser at a powder rather than liquid.

However, in the infancy stage, most of the technologies had their deficiencies. They had some imperfections. Some of the deficiencies include the hardening of the materials as a result of some warping in them and the high cost of the machines for home inventors. One can say these deficiencies, and many more contributed to the need to keep working on it, which will lead to the next stage – the adolescent stage.

The Adolescent Stage

The adolescent stage was between 1999 and 2010. The year 1999 was the wake of the period when the first 3D-printed organ was implanted in humans. The activities of the scientists at Wake Forest Institute for Regenerative Medicine led to the printing of synthetic scaffolds of a human bladder and its coating with the cells of humans. A new tissue was generated, and they implanted the tissue into a human patient. The patient's immune systems didn't reject the tissue since it was made from their cells. The adolescent stage had space in the field of medicine as scientists from various startups and institutions came together and fabricated a functional miniature kidney, they built a prosthetic leg, using complex components printed from the same structure, they also had bioprinting of the first blood vessels using the human cells only.

Similarly, at this stage, the 3D printing met the open-source movement. Dr. Adrian Bowyer was engaged in

RepRap Project, and in 2005, this project launched an open-source initiative, which was geared toward building a 3D printer that could build itself or probably print most of its parts. In 2008, the project was achieved with the release of Darwin, which is a self-replicating printer. With this new stride in the 3D industry and technology, people earned the ability to create whatsoever idea they had a dream.

The democratization of manufacturing captured many people's imagination, and it has engrafted the idea of mass customization as well. In 2006, the first SLS machine became viable commercially, and this opened the opportunity for on-demand manufacturing of industrial parts. A machine with the capacity to print in multiple materials was created by a 3D startup *Objet*, which is presently merged with *Stratasys*. The machine paved the way for one part to be fabricated in various versions using different material properties.

The crux of the adolescent stage, where there was a show of creativity in innovation at its peak, was the launch of collaborative co-creation services, including Shapeways. Shapeways is a 3D-printing marketplace that creates a platform for designers to receive feedback from consumers and possibly from other designers. It also makes it possible for designers to fabricate their products at affordable prices. Later, MakerBot also came up to the market, and it offers open-source DIY kits for designers to create their 3D printers and products. With these innovations, inventors and designers were facing lesser barriers in their process of entering the 3D printing market.

The Maturity/Prime Stage

When one looks back into the previous ages of 3D printing, he or she would observe a significant change that has occurred over the years. There has been consistency fall in the price of 3D printers over the years, while the accuracy and effectiveness of the machines have greatly increased. Beyond the dream of Charles Hull, many innovators had worked on 3D printers to make it achieve a new height. Presently, designing is not limited to the use of plastic. However, different objects can have something printed on them. You can have a ring with printing on it either in gold or silver. Among the new innovations the 3D printing has experienced, there is the first 3D-printed unmanned aircraft, which was flown by engineers at the University of Southampton, and a car that has a 3D-printed body. It was built to acquire 200mpg on the freeway.

More than the aforementioned, 3D printing in the Prime stage has encompassed more functions and use. It helps to create affordable housing in the developing world. Other scientists are making use of it to print other things, including smart robotic arms, bone replacements, and particles that are as thick as an atom; these particles are useful in creating smaller electronics and batteries. One other thing worthy of note about 3D printing is that it is a technological reality that is not staying. Rather, it is making a move to keep revolving and becoming generally acceptable and relevant in different fields and areas of study.

How 3D printing Works

All 3D printers you see build parts following a specific principle. The principle guiding their working is this: a digital model becomes a three-dimensional object through the addition of materials in layers. It works differently from CNC machining, which is the traditional subtractive, and formative, which is an Injection molding; both were the conventional manufacturing technologies that 3D printing came to displace. For 3D printing, the designer doesn't need to get any special tools, such as mold or geometry. Rather the designer builds the parts directly on the built platform in layers. With this method, there are specific benefits and limitations. To start the 3D printing process, there will be a digital 3D model. This 3D model is the blueprint of the object you want to see. For the printer to work effectively, and carry out production, it works with set of instructions that are in form of a machine language (G-code). The printer gets its G-code from the model by slicing it to 2-dimensional layers, which ends up being converted into the language the machine understands.

Creating A 3D Model

The 3D can be created by the designer or downloaded from a 3D repository. To create a 3D model, you can use an app, haptic device, 3D scanner, or a 3D modeling software. There are lots of 3D modeling software tools you can get. There are varieties: industrial grade and open-source software. For the industrial-grade software, it will cost thousands of dollars annually for each license, while the open-source is free.

As a starter, you can lay your hands on Tinkercad. It is open-source software, and it works easily in any browser without installing it. The software has a free lesson package for users ay the beginner level. Also, it offers a built-in feature that makes it easier to have your 3D model printed through a 3D print service. After you have successfully created the 3D model, the next step is to create a slicing. Slicing refers to the preparation of the file for your 3D printer

Slicing Your 3D Model

In the process of slicing, you will be dividing your 3D model into many (ranging from hundreds to thousands) horizontal layers using a slicing software. It is possible to have a 3D printer that has a custom-made slicer. Such a 3D printer will give room to feed the raw. Or the CAD file. Feeding your 3D model is what happens when you have successfully sliced it. You feed your 3D model to your 3D printer. Feeding the 3D model is done through USB, SD, or the internet. Once it is fed, you can print your 3D model in layers.

There are variations in the process 3D printers undergo to function. A desktop FDM, for instance, works by melting plastic filaments, and it lay it down on the print platform via a nozzle – it is like a computer-controlled glue gun. Large industrial SLS machines, they make use of a laser to melt thin layers of plastic powders or metal. Also, the process involved makes the materials vary. Commonly, one would find plastic, while metals can also have 3D print on them. There is the possibility of a wide-range of certain properties, such as optical clarity, and rubber-like look.

In the working of a 3d printer, there is a distinction in the time of its operation. The size of a 3D printer's part and its own type determine how long it will take to complete a particular printing. Usually, the hours range from 4 to 18 hours. It is rare to find a ready-to-use printed part of any machine. There is usually the need to undergo some post-processing to achieve a surface you wish. However, this processing takes additional time.

CHAPTER TWO

KNOWING MORE ABOUT THE TECHNOLOGY DEVICE 1

Just as it is for every other business, it is quite important for anyone who wishes to do 3D printing business to understand everything that needs to be understood about 3D printing. In this chapter and the next chapters, I will be explicating on every aspect of 3D printing that you need to know before you place your next investment into it.

USES OF 3D PRINTING: INDUSTRIAL AND PERSONAL USE

3D printing has gained wide recognition. This recognition has given it an envious market that is ready to make millionaires out of anyone who wishes to utilize the opportunity. The real winner of this reality is the usefulness of 3D printing itself. For every business that has come to stay in our world today, they share something in common – a willingness to solve people's problems. Similarly, 3D printing is not one-sided. It operates in such a way that it is useful both industrially and personally. The universality of its functions plays a key role in its wide acceptance.

The Industrial Uses

3D printing gained its influence by being a useful tool for industries. It makes it possible for manufacturers to exercise a large percentage of control over their inventory via its two basic applications, which are rapid prototyping, and rapid manufacturing. Rapid prototyping makes it possible for industries to design their products using the printer. The design is known as the prototype, which industries create using modeling software, and then send it to the printer rather than sending it to a manufacturer that is off-site, which often takes weeks for them to receive the product. 3D printing makes it possible for industries to create a prototype and print it at the same time. This saves time and money. Also, on the aspect of rapid manufacturing, 3D printing makes it possible for industries to produce the needed amount of products at a particular point in time. That is, when a business needs to produce a little number of custom products, it makes it possible for the business not to have mass production. The printer in this scenario builds the finished products, not a prototype. The industrial use of 3D printing is in different fields. I will discuss some of the common sectors or industries where 3D printing is often utilized in a later chapter.

The Personal Uses

Aside from industrial use, 3D printing also finds its way into the daily activities of everyone. The universality of a 3D printer is replicated in the fact that it is not restricted to the printing of a specific object. Unlike a normal desktop printer, which is designed to print papers, a 3D printer is designed for different roles at various capacities. It can be used by startup companies to develop and test a product. This will empower the company to carry out any kink in design at the beginning of production. You can get custom solutions, such as personalized wine rack, or an edgy flower vase for your house through creative DIY. You may also use it to aid your children's study. When you tinker with a 3D printer, your kid can learn simple design principles and engineering techniques.

Just as architects make use of the 3D printer to create models in order to visualize their designs, kids can also create models of different atomic structures. These structures will explain to them some of the basics of chemistry that they need to understand. Also, it will explain to them how the different parts fit together. Thus, the educational foundation of your kids would be strengthened. Another set of people that often utilize 3D printing is Artists. They make use of the 3D printer to create models and sculptures. They are able to do this by fusing the ancient art of sculpting and digital design and 3D printing.

3D PRINTING VERSUS THE TRADITIONAL MANUFACTURING METHOD

Recently, 3D printing has gained grounds in the manufacturing industries. It has the capacity to manufacture on a wider scale within a short period. As I mentioned in the previous chapter that 3D printing has been in vogue over the years; also, there has been a constant improvement in it. Thus improvement has made it become lower in cost while it maintains its effectiveness; hence, the need for more companies to subscribe to it. The 3D process of assembling a new object in layers through the use of specialized equipment is quite advantageous over the traditional method of manufacturing. I will take you through the observable differences between 3D printing and the traditional method of production.

Producing Prototype

Making a prototype using 3D printing is quite easier, faster, and cheaper compared to the traditional method of manufacturing. The 3D printing, in general, does not seek any special tooling in the production of a part, unlike the traditional method that often requires more effort on tooling the production line, and setting up the assembly process that will be utilized for production.

If there is a mistake in the process of production, and the design requires a rework, it is faster to reprogram the design into the 3D printer and reprint the real design. However, a traditional manufacturing method requires you to retool the line to remove some handful of prototype parts, and this wastes time, labor, and material. 3D printing is the best when the production of a limited-run prototype of a part is concerned.

Preventing Waste of Resources

One other essential advantage of 3D printing over the traditional method of production is its high level of resource management. In the 3D printer, you not need many materials. The material that is used up is that which goes through the extruder of the 3D printer for the building of the object. The traditional method, such as the injection-mode, requires more materials to make sure the mold is filled up. When perforated sheet metal assembly processes are involved, a lot of sheet metal is required, with holes cut into them. Whatever materials that were used to fill those holes earlier becomes useless as scraps. Well, the scraps can be recycled. However, the process is demanding and laborious.

Usually, in the production process, 3D printing produces fewer scraps than traditional manufacturing methods. Also, with 3D printing, it is not a must for producers to produce in mass before he or she can justify the setup cost. Unlike the traditional supply chain that relies greatly on the effectiveness of mass productions, with the need for a large number of assembly workers, additive manufacturing requires fewer materials to carry out any production or the blueprint, which is the model to carry out its production.

Producing in large scale

The additive manufacturing is quite less effective when large scale production is involved. After creating the model or prototype, producing at a very high speed in large quantities will be inadequate on the 3D printer, while the traditional methods would be more reliable with respect to that. Although the 3D printer does not require retooling as the production is ongoing, however, the process of assembling an object in a 3D printer is quite pale in comparison to the conventional manufacturing methods.

The delay is a result of the need for a 3D printer to assemble an object in layers, with a layer coming before the next, by placing a new layer on the previous one. The fastest 3D printer will still take quite some hours to make a small object. For example, making a pair of nutcrackers on the 3D printer would take up to 3 hours. When the same object is made using the injection molding, a traditional method, dozens of the nutcracker would be produced within the same amount of time. Hence, 3D printing has a shorter lead time. However, the traditional manufacturing method is faster in speed when mass production is involved.

Creation of Unique Materials

The latest development in 3D printing, including Selective Laser Sintering, has made it possible to create new objects from new and special materials such as polymers and some metals. Nonetheless, to create objects from these special materials, a special 3d printer designed for the materials is required. There are also materials that cannot work with the 3D printer, such as some metal alloys due to their high melting points. This seems to be a limitation whenever there is a need for certain materials for a particular part of the object.

Parts production Scale

3D printing has challenges with the production of some specific large-scale parts, unlike the traditional method of production. The total area of the printing bed decides the scale of any part to be produced. The model of your 3D printer, then, decides the size of the parts to be produced, which could be some cubic inches or cubic feet.

3D gives the opportunity to create parts in different pieces for you to assemble later; however, that may not be suitable. It will lead to the use of labor for the final stage of building the object, which goes against the low labor use advantage it has, and it can also lead to stress points in some parts that require solidification so they can work at peak performance.

Having looked at these differences and specific effects of the 3D printing and traditional method of manufacturing, one tends to start ruminating on the best method of manufacturing. However, the truth remains that 3D printing doesn't seem to have what it takes to replace the traditional method of manufacturing any moment soon completely. Rather, it possesses an incredible utility for one-off production runs. It is also great for the production of small custom workpieces that would originally require a lot of specialized tooling to produce. 3D printing for most industries is not to replace the traditional manufacturing method but to augment their traditional production processes and increase their abilities to provide a fast and well-made object to their customers. 3D printing serves the function of expanding the production capabilities of those companies that use it.

THE FUTURE OF 3D PRINTING

Looking beyond the present realities and pressing further into what the future holds, one would see a brighter beam of hope for 3D printing in our world. The future of 3D printing lies in the kind of hope it promises to give us. Just imagine you printing a toy that your kid designed for him or her. With the present printing of necessary organs in the hospitals, there will be lost of waiting lists for those who are interested in organ transplants, thus, saving many lives. There is an expectation for a great change in space exploration as Astronauts will have the capacity to make parts as demanded. For any medical or technical equipment, they have it within their caprices, with the need for just a desktop printer.

There will be a change in the approach of consumers that use the 3D printer in their bid to access and customize products. Rather than contacting the producer to order new parts for their cars, or any other gadgets, the consumer can easily identify the right design file by checking the website of the company, and download it, and take the next step which is to print it immediately. With this possibility, there will be no need to wait endlessly for products or parts. Whenever a person comes across a product, he or she would be able to print it out without waiting for shipping, and saving extra charges on shipping, while he or she enjoys the product instantly. Presently, we are all witnessing the exciting opportunities that 3D printing has to offer. Though many people are yet to recognize the full potential of the technology, nonetheless, the move of many companies into a digital and smarter manufacturing model will, in no time, reveal the relevance of 3D printing more and more.

THE IMPORTANCE OF 3D PRINTING

One question I have always heard people ask about 3D printing is: what importance does it have? What are its advantages? And what are the limitation affecting it? To some people, they have a side of them that tells them it is a fad. That is, it is an area of interest for technologists and inventors. However, many people will not have a need for it or make use of it. The reason for this misunderstanding about 3D's importance is not farfetched. It has been a companion to many engineers and designers for over three decades, and it is only gaining wide knowledge recently. So, to many people, the machines seem to have sprouted out of nowhere and gained grounds. It has become accessible, and everyone now has a glimpse of what a 3D printer does.

Its recent growth is owing to the significant decrease in its price that happened over the last years. And with the innovative work of some companies, which have led to the building of modern desktop versions of the conventional industrial-sized machines. This innovation made additive manufacturing machines affordable and available for consumers who are interested in creativity and value its use. The importance of 3D printing lies in its ability to transform consumerism. There is a possibility of entirely new customization and an important shift in production power through the empowering of people to create their goods. Below are the realities that talk about the importance of additive manufacturing machines.

Healthcare Innovations

The Importance of 3D printing is not farfetched. It is evident in the different ways it is used nowadays. Looking into the healthcare system, there are a lot of uses for 3D printing by this sector. In the surgery unit of medicine, surgeons are hinging the plans of their operations on 3D printing. They will use it to produce replicas of the physical issues they are operating on. These printed replicas are what they will review for further works. This move will give surgeons a great level of idea of what the surgeries entail, which reduces the possibility of running into an error while the operation is on. Aside from its importance in medical practice, it is also important in medical studies. Medical students can learn human anatomy better at a cost-effective rate with printed models. Rather than gathering cadavers for their studies, medical schools now print models. One other area in healthcare that the additive manufacturing machine has proved its importance is in the treatment of prosthetic limbs. There are many prosthetic limbs developed via 3D printing, and this has made many people have access to the care regardless of their background since it is now affordable.

Fashion and Design Innovations

It is a key tool for designers (fashion and interior) to create new innovative products. Through 3D printing, fashion has ventured into the production of high heels of different styles, and jewelry of great tastes. It is now so easy for interior designers to create ottomans, beautiful tables, and chairs in sets. There is now an observable artistic beautifying of furniture than the popular conventional ones. The furniture designs from 3D printing are lighter than their traditional counterparts, as well; they are leek and durable. Beyond furniture, lamps have also enjoyed the beautifying strength of 3D printing. There are many lamps – floor lamp, ceiling light, table lamp, and wall lamp, being printed and designed via the additive machines.

Its Importance to Inventors and DIY

3D printing takes its importance a step further to inventors and DIY enthusiasts. DIY refers to those who believe in doing things themselves; hence, the term, "Do it Yourself." Inventors and DIY make use of the machine to bring their ideas and wish to reality by making a solid object from their ideas. 3D printing offers the possibility of spending less by printing a prototype of an idea or product, which costs less than creating a product by hand or giving it out to a manufacturer to produce. This makes it easier for inventors to quickly make a design prototype of a product and test it before the real production at a low cost. The cost of producing an item using 3D is far lesser than the cost using the traditional way.

In addition, designers and inventors are able to keep their ideas confidential since the 3D printer can be used at home; hence, this helps to deal with the risk of having their works imitated. Also, a person may decide to share his or her digital print model online for people that are likeminded to go through, review, and possibly improve on.

Also, more than printing and testing product models, 3D printers helps to make products that one can deliver. As a result of mass production, there is less availability of customized toys, and when there is one, it tends to be expensive; however, a 3D printer is one thing you need to make that specially designed product for yourself.

Its Importance for Personal Use

The additive manufacturing machine has left the shore of industries into the domestic domain. You would be surprised seeing how practical it is in doing certain tasks within the house. It is used to print custom doorstops, corner buffers, and bookends. It makes it easier for people to design products for their personal needs. Prior to now, there were lots of images and virtual objects created digitally through designing. However, these images were restricted to being viewed on screens but were not printed and put to use. 3D printing has made this a reality. Everyone can now create a design of them from their idea using a modeling program and have it printed in less than a full day.

The additive manufacturing machine has made artists and designer's virtual world created to become a reality. Sculpture works, and figurines do not have to undergo the traditional method of production anymore. There is the possibility of testing the various look and feel of sculptors and figurines by artists before the final production.

THE ADVANTAGES OF 3D PRINTING

More than its importance, there are certain benefits attached to 3D printing. The creation of parts via creating layers one at a time fully explains 3D printing. This method of production gives it its advantages over the traditional methods. When you have a full understanding of the benefits and advantages that come with 3D printing, you would be able to make the best decision when you select a manufacturing process or make use of the 3D printer to deliver optimal services and products to your clients. Below are the advantages of the 3D printer:

It is Fast

Can you imagine creating an idea in your head overnight and have it in your hand before dusk? This possibility is one of the key advantages of the additive manufacturing method. Once you upload a complex design from a CAD model into the 3D printer, you will have your product in a few hours. There is a very rapid process of verifying and developing design ideas when

3D is involved. Whereas, in the conventional methods, it takes days, and at times, weeks to have a prototype at hand. The prototype gets into the hands of the designer in a few hours using the additive method. The 3D printer has the ability to produce functional end parts at a low to mid-volume, and this gives it its time-saving advantage.

Easy One-Step Production

One of the biggest concerns for a designer is how to manufacture a part as efficiently as possible. Most parts require a large number of manufacturing steps to be produced by traditional technologies. The order these steps occur affects the quality and manufacturability of the design. It has a one-way method of production, with the CAD model coming first. After creating the design, the next step is to carry out the fabrication by cutting the steel profiles to size. Afterward, you will then have to clamp the profiles into positions, while you weld them one after the other to create the bracket shape.

You may have to make a custom jig to make sure that all components aligned correctly. You will then polish the welds to make it have a beautiful surface when it is finished. You will then drill the next holes to mount the bracket on the wall. Finally, the bracket will be sandblasted, primed, and painted to make I have a more beautiful appearance.

Using additive manufacturing is straightforward. There is no interaction from the machine operator during the process of building. Once you are done with the CAD design, you can upload it to the machine and print it out in a single step within a few hours. The possibility of a single step means of production greatly nullifies the need to depend on various production procedures such as welding, machining, and painting. This gives the designer a great control over the product produced.

It is cost-effective

Cost is an important part of the production. In 3D printing, the cost of manufacturing can be divided into three categories: the cost of machine operation, the material cost, and the labor cost. I will be looking at them one after the other.

The cost of machine operation: the cost of machine operation for 3D printing has a low significance on the overall cost a production requires. This is because many of the 3D printers require a similar amount of power just as a laptop. For the industrial additive manufacturing technology, there is a need for a high amount of energy to produce a part; nonetheless, the possibility of creating some complex geometries within a single step leads to a high level of efficiency and turnaround.

Material cost: there are distinctions in the material cost for additive manufacturing depending on the technology. For example, the SLA printing needs resin that is close to $150 per liter, while the Desktop FDM printer makes use of filament coils that goes for $25 per kg. It is difficult to have a quantifiable comparison of additive manufacturing and traditional manufacturing due to the range of materials that are available for additive manufacturing. The SLS makes use of nylon powder, and this powder costs around $70 per kg, on the other hand, an injection molding uses nylon pellets, which goes for as low as $2 to $5 per kg. The cost of materials has a great impact on the cost of producing a part using additive manufacturing.

Labor cost: there is the low cost of labor in additive manufacturing. Aside from the post-processing, most of the 3D printers require just n operator to press a button on the printer. The printer works with an automated process in the production of the part. When you compare 3D printing to traditional manufacturing, which requires the service of highly skilled engineers to man the machines, the labor cost of 3D printing is nothing; it would even be safe to say that 3D printing requires no labor.

There are lots of competition as to the low rate of production in additive manufacturing, unlike traditional manufacturing. One way to prove this is the clear difference between the cost of making prototypes used to ascertain the form and fitting of products and that of other ways of manufacturing, including injection molding. At the same time, this model is highly competitive for producing one-off parts. Traditional manufacturing only becomes more cost-effective when the number of production increases. To justify the high amount of setup, there must be a large quantity of production.

It mitigates Risk

Risk is an important aspect of every business venture. In 3D printing, once you order a faulty prototype, you are risking both your time and money. In fact, a little modification to mold or fabrication can have a great level of financial implications. The possibility of creating a prototype, and verifying a design before you put in your money into real production is a great way 3D printing has come to help mitigate a great risk. The design model you create will help to build your trust and confidence in your design and product before you place all your investment into the mass production of the product.

It gives Design freedom

The traditional manufacturing placed a lot of restrictions on what a person can make. However, additive manufacturing does not set any barrier. The process of 3D printing, which is produced in layers, makes the need for certain requirements such as draft angles, tools access, and undercut needless. Although 3D printing gives limitations on the minimum size of parts that can be printed, the restrictions are geared toward having an optimal orientation of a print, in order to avoid the print failure and reduce the need for support dependency. With this, every designer has a lot of freedom to design and can make complex geometries easily.

It gives room for Customization

Aside from the freedom of design, it gives to every designer, 3D printing makes it possible for designers and DIY to customize their designs. The technology is perfect at single building parts each at a given time; this makes it suitable for one-off production. This benefit is what medical practitioners and industries have embraced and utilized. They have developed custom implants, prosthetics, and dental aids. There is also high-level sporting gear created to fit a specific athlete. These gear include custom sunglasses and other fashion accessories. With additive manufacturing, you can produce a single custom part at a cheap rate.

It gives Ease of Access

There has been a major growth of additive manufacturing in the last nine years. This growth is owed to the availability of the 3D printers in the market in a large number. As a result, many designers have access to additive manufacturing technology. According to a report (Wohler's report, 2015), over 278,000 additive manufacturing printers, which worth $5000, were bought globally in the year 2015. There has been a double increase in the number sold annually afterward. Initially, it was only made available to a few people; however, now, it is available to a wider range of users, including industries.

It is Sustainable

The Subtractive manufacturing method, which was a traditional manufacturing method, removes a large number of materials from an original block during production, which results in a high quantity of material wastage. However, for additive manufacturing, only the material that is required to build a part is used. In the process of production, 3D printing often uses raw material that can be recycled and reused; hence, there is a less quantity of material wastage in additive manufacturing.

The distance of shipping prototype parts has been greatly impacted by the increase in the volume of additive manufacturing machines in the market globally. There is a small learning curve in every tabletop 3D printer, and this curve is what makes it easier to operate the machine successfully; hence, many designers do not take their designs to expert in manufacturing industries any more to be produced. As a result, there are many 3D printing businesses globally regardless of the location, and the high cost of land. The significant reduction in shipping requirement impacts the environment positively, and the possibility of printing and producing parts on-site birth smaller carbon footprint for many parts that are produced through additive manufacturing.

CHAPTER THREE

THE LIMITATIONS

The additive manufacturing technology has certain limitations that serve as its disadvantages. It is equally important for you to understand these deficiencies so as to understand fully how the machine works in full.

It has a lower strength and anisotropic material properties

In general, additive manufacturing parts are not strong enough in their physical properties. Their fragility is a result of the layers they are made of. The physical properties are weaker and brittle in a direction with a 10% to 50% approximation. As a result, when non-critical functional applications are involved, the plastic 3D printed parts are used. Nonetheless, there are machines, such as DML and SLM, that can produce metal 3D printed parts that possess perfect mechanical properties, which is quite better than the bulk material. As a result, these machines have been applied in certain industries, such as aerospace.

There is a need for post-processing and support removal

It is often rare to have a printed part that is ready to use once it leaves the printer. There is usually a need for one or more post-processing steps to be taken. For instance, most 3D printing processes always require support removal. Additive manufacturing does not have the capacity to add material on thin air. Thus, support is used to add material under an overhang or to serve as an anchor for the printed part on the build platform. When supports are removed, they leave blemishes on the surface of the part they were used with. The area where they were removed will then need extra operations such as smoothing, sanding and painting to have a perfect surface.

There is less cost-competition as quantity increases

Unlike the traditional manufacturing process that gives a lesser price as the quantity to be produced increases, 3D printing does not give a great deal of reduction in the prices when the volume of production increases. There is no custom tool or mold. Hence it is cheap for startups costs, and a small number of parts can be produced at a very cheap rate. However, once the quantity increases, the price of production only decreases slightly. At the level of mass production, traditional technologies such as the CNC machining and injection molding are more cost-effective.

It has limited accuracy and tolerance

The calibration of the machine and the process of production determine the accuracy of additive manufacturing technology. Every part printed on a desktop FDM printer has the lowest accuracy and prints with the tolerance rate of ± 0.5 mm. The implication of this is that if a hole is designed with a 10mm diameter, the real diameter it will bring out after printing will be between 9.5mm and 10.5mm. However, every other 3D printing process gives better accuracy. If you are using an industrial material jetting or SLA printer, you will be able to produce products down to ± 0.1 mm. However, note that you can only get this result once you have optimized for certain features in a well-designed part. If you are dealing with metal 3D printed parts, you need the CNC machining to finish it for a critical application, or probably, you take it through a new process after printing, in order to improve its tolerance and its surface look.

TYPES OF THE TECHNOLOGY DEVICE

The additive manufacturing technology is a tech for everyone who loves interactive technology and is easy to use at the same time. From the inception in 1983 when an American inventor Charles Hull came up with physical evidence of how possible it is to have a 3D printing, the technology has gained wide acceptance among many innovators, and hence, gone beyond the stereolithography (SLA) apparatus product of Charles. Over the years, there have been new innovations based on different factors and circumstances, and these innovations have birth newer forms of 3D printers.

Presently, we have different types of 3D printers globally; however, despite their differences, they share similar printing processes. Six basic factors or better still, considerations were crucial for the differences in 3D printers. The factors are the quality of printing, the speed of printing, the cost of the printer, the capability of a printer, the practicality of printer, and the expectations of users.

Some printers are designed to print text only, while some print both graphics and text. Also, there are variations in the materials and the technologies used. 3D printers are quite smarter than traditional manufacturing technology, and 3D printers give a different range of offers, including materials, quality, and price. At the end of this chapter, you would have widened your knowledge with the understanding of all the different types of 3D printers you can lay your hand on in the market. While you prepare to invest in a 3D printer, the knowledge you gather from here will guide you to make a well-informed decision before you invest that hard-earned money.

Right before I start discussing the different types of 3D printer you can get, I will take you through the basic components of the additive manufacturing machine. The 3D printer is made up of many parts, which are all crucial to its effective operation. The main components are basically what I will explain here so as to aid your understanding of how they function in the different types. The following are the basic components of an additive manufacturing machine and their functions:

3D Printer Frame: this frame serves as a binding agent that holds the machine together.

3D Printer Head movement mechanics: it moves in relation to the print bed in every direction.

3D printer Head: it is the nozzle that gives filament or adds colors and a liquid binder.

3D Build Platform or Build Bed: this is the part of the printer where the object is printed.

3D Printer Stepper Motors (there are at least four): they operate for positioning rightly and controlling speed.

3D Printer Electronics: it is used for driving motors, to heat the extruder, and so on.

3D Printer Firmware: it is the software (Permanent) of the machine that is utilized to control all other segments of the machine.

3D Printer Software: the software is not a physical component of the printer. However, it serves a great deal in the process of printing.

Aside from these physical components, there are certain support substances that work with 3D printers to function effectively. These substances are used to support complex geometries. Just like the real base materials, the support materials are also important in the process of 3D printing. When there is no support, the printing will not come out well. Unlike the traditional physical support used in traditional manufacturing, the new materials for support for 3D printing offer a better solution. At the end of the production, the designer can remove all support substances from the finished product. Also, note that some 3D machines make use of support materials that dissolve once they get into a chemical bath. For some, they make use of the surrounding powder to make everything stay put, while there are some that use a squidgy, gel-like substance.

Basically, there are nine types of 3D printer. All of these types have their names lengthy. However, they all possess an acronym. In the course of this chapter, I will make use of their acronyms to refer to them more in order to hasten your reading.

The Stereolithography Technology (SLA)

The SLA machine involves a fast prototyping process. It is often used by those who are interested in accuracy and precision. The machine often produces an object from 3D CAD data, which is computer-generated files within a couple of hours. The SLA is well known for its well-detailed printing and exactness. The products of this technology are usually unique in their models, prototype, patterns, and other production parts. The machine works by converting liquid photopolymers, which is a unique plastic kind to a solid 3D object in layers. The process of converting the plastic involves heating the plastic to make it turn to a semi-liquid form, and it ends up hardening as it comes in contact. The layers in the object are constructed by the printer through the use of an ultraviolet laser that is placed under the direction of X and Y scanning mirrors. There is a recoater blade that works by moving across the object before each circle of the printing. The recoater moves to make sure that each thin layer of resin spreads evenly across the object. This process is followed for each printing done on the 3D printer to build any new object.

Once the object is formed, a person will take it away from the printer and detach it with care from the platform. If there is excess resin, there is a chemical bath on the 3D part that is meant to remove the excess resin. You may also take the object through post-processing by post-curing it in an ultraviolet oven. The post-curing renders the object stronger and stable. Some parts may have to go through the process of hand sanding and painting. For most industries, they prefer the SLA machine. It is an economical choice for many industries such as aerospace, entertainment, automotive, medical, and other industries that are into the production of consumer products. The SLA machine has a lot of printers that benefit from its technology. These printers include, but not limited to, XYZ printing Nobel 1.0 SLA 3D printer, Form 1+ SLA 3D Printer, SUNLU SLA Desktop 3D Printer, etc.

The Digital Light Processing (DLP) Technology

One of the oldest 3D printing technologies of the 80s is DLP. It performs similarly to SLA, by working with photopolymers also. There is a translucent resin container that receives the liquid plastic resin that the printer uses during operation. However, the source of light for SLA and DLP serves as the distinguishing factor between them. For SLA, its source of light is the ultraviolet light, while DLP gains its light from a traditional source, especially lamps. As a result, the printing process of DLP is fast. One the light intensifies, the resin hardens quickly within seconds. Unlike the SLA printing process, DLP prints faster for most parts. The WHY of this is because DLP exposes all the layers at the same time. Unlike SLA printing that requires a laser first to draw out each of the layers, which takes quite a lot of time.

Another interesting fact about DLP technology is its robust efficiency. For every production, the object enjoys a very high-resolution model each time. Also, it is cost-effective and economical in expenses. It is designed to use cheap materials for any kind of object printing, including complex and detailed objects. As a result of this, there is a low wastage of materials, as well as a reduction in the cost of production. The DLP printer has a wide range of machines that makes use of its technology. Some of them are Desktop UV DLP, LumiPocket – Miniature DLP, Makes M-one Desktop DLP 3D Printer, etc.

The Fused Deposition Modeling (FDM) Technology

The FDM technology was introduced in the 1980s. Scott Crump did its inception conception, but it was later implemented by Stratasys Ltd. The FDM makes use of grade thermal plastic materials during production to make 3D prints. The technology is notable for making models of concepts, prototypes that are useful and functional, and in the production of manufacturing aids. It creates well-detailed objects and offers great strength at the weight ratio.

FDM printing has pre-print activities. Before you start printing, you need to slice the 3D CAD data, which is the 3D model into a lot of layers via special software. It is the sliced CAD that will go into the printer and start building the object in layers, one at a time on the build platform. The process of building is done by heating and extruding the thermoplastic filament via the nozzle and then on the base. The FDM printer has the capacity to extrude different support materials, including thermoplastic. The printer, at times in the process of supporting an upper layer, may add certain support material underneath. This material will later dissolve after the printing process. The FDM printing time depends on the size of the object and how complex the object is, just as it is for every other 3D printer.

The FDM printer's final product often requires cleaning. A raw FDM Part may show visible layer-lines on some objects. When such occurs, the object requires hand sanding and finishing after printing it. The hand sanding and finishing will smoothen it and give it an even surface. One key benefit of FDM printed objects is that they are durable and functional. Hence, it has been widely accepted by most industries, including parts manufacturers and mechanical engineers. For instance, the automobile industry BMW uses FDM 3D printing, so also is Nestle, among many others. Talking of popular FDM printers, we have ALUNAR High-Resolution Desktop FDM 3D Printer, Original Prusa i3 MK2, PowerSpec 3D Pro, FlashForge Creator Pro, etc.

The Selective Laser Sintering (SLS) Technology

The mid-1980s made a great contribution to the market of 3D printing with the introduction of the Selective Laser Sintering Technology by an American businessman, inventor, and teacher, Dr. Carl Deckard.

Deckard developed and patented the SLS technology. The SLS technology is a 3D printing machine that makes use of powerful CO_2 lasers to join particles. Usually, the laser sinters turn metal materials to powder; it, however, has the capacity to make use of other materials such as white nylon powder, glass, and ceramics also.

The SLS process involves the incrementally lowering of the build bed with each successive laser scan. This process occurs with each layer until it finally gets to the height of the object. The model is surrounded and protected during the building process by un-sintered support that is gained from other powders. As a result, there is no need for other support for the object under print during the production process. Immediately after printing, someone needs to remove the un-sintered powders manually from the build bed. The object produced from SLS is usually durable, has high precision parts, and is universal in its choice of materials. The SLS technology works perfectly for end-use parts and prototypes that are functional .it shares certain features with SLA technology in relation to quality and speed. However, they use different materials. SLS technology makes use of powdered substances, while SLA embraces liquid resins. The resins are what makes SLA technology stands out as the best 3D printing process for customized objects.

The Selective Laser Melting (SLM) Technology

The SLM technology came into existence in 1995 as part of research in a German college, Fraunhofer Institute ILT in Aachen. The SLM shares similarly feature with SLA. It uses a high-powered laser beam to make 3D objects. In the course of production, the laser beam is responsible for melting and joining different metallic powders to combine together. The process has a formula or a process method. It is in this form:

(Powdered material) + (heat) +(precision) + (layered structure) = a perfect 3D object

Once the laser beam meets a thin layer of the material, it will weld the particles together in a selective manner. Once a cycle has been printed, the printer will add another layer of powered material to the previously printed layer. At this time, the object will lower by the precise amount of a single layer's thickness. Once the production process is completed, a person will have to remove the powder that is not used from the object manually. The aspect of differences between SLM and SLS is in their methods of melting the powder. While SLM melts the powder completely, SLS melts the powder partially. Typically, the Object that is produced from SLM ends up becoming stronger since there are fewer or possibly no voids in it.

The Selective laser melting technology is often used for the printing of 3D objects that have complex structures, geometries, and thin walls. The aerospace is another industry that makes good use of the SLM technology in its projects. The reason for its use is because it gives precision, durability, and lightweight to whatever object it creates. However, SLM is quite expensive. Hence it is not common among domestic users. Nonetheless, it is a favorite of many industries, including the aerospace and medical orthopedics. Many researchers, universities, and metal powder developers are consistently investing in SLM 3D printers. Among the SLM 3d printers, there are Realizer SLM 125, SLM Solutions SLM 125, 280, and 500, etc.

The Electron Beam Melting (EBM) Technology

The Electron beam melting technology was a brainchild of a Swedish company – Arcam AB in the year 1997. The 3D printer shares specific features with the SLM by using a powder bed fusion method. However, it makes use of a different power source. The SLM technology utilizes a high-powered laser in a noble chamber, or inert gas, while the EBM makes use of a powerful electron that is in a vacuum. Every other thing, aside from the power source, is similar. The Electron beam melting technology is basically used for printing metal parts in 3D format. It is characterized by the ability to carry out complex geometries. The parts that EBM produces are often strong and dense in their makeup. The technology has various impressive features such as the following:

It does not require extra auxiliary tools in the process of 3D printing.

When raw materials are used, it has increased efficiency.

There is a lesser amount of lead time, and this makes it faster for the produced parts to get to market.

It has the capability to make parts that are functional, durable, and that are on a wide range of demand by industries.

Just like every other printing technology, it also starts with the creation of a 3D model or CAD, which is a digital file generated by the computer. Arcam Q20 is an EBM printer that is efficient for industrial use.

The Laminated Object Manufacturing (LOM) Technology

The Laminated object manufacturing technology was developed by a Californian company – Helisys Inc. (now called Cubic Technologies). It was developed as an affordable and efficient 3D printing method. With the input of an American engineer – Michael Feygin, the LOM was patented to him. The LOM works through heat and pressure. It works through fusion, and lamination of paper or plastic layers under heat and pressure. There is an automated blade or laser that is responsible for cutting the objects to the shape the designer wishes. After completing a layer, the platform then moves downward by about 1/16thinch to start the next layer. To start a new layer, the printer will pull a new material sheet across the substrate, where it is adhered to by a heated roller. This process is what goes on over and over until the product is finally produced.

To have a better understanding of how it works, you can go through the following.

The sheet is made to stay to a substrate with a heated roller

The laser traces your desired prototype dimensions

The laser will cross hatches non-part area so as to remove waste.

Every platform that has a completed layer will move down out of the way

Then new material sheet will be rolled into position

, and the platform will go down to form a new position so it can receive a new layer

The process will be repeated.

LOM is one of the fastest 3D printing technology today. Among the numerous technology for prototyping, it is probably the most affordable. The affordability is due to the low cost of materials it requires, that is the papers and plastics. Also, the LOM creates quite large 3D objects. It has its relevance among artists, product developers, and architects. The Mcor Matrix is one of the most popular LOM printers.

The Binder Jetting (BJ) Technology

The foremost academic center of technology, Massachusetts Institute of Technology (MIT), was the pioneer of the BJ 3D technology. It is also called the inkjet 3D printing, powder bed printing, and Drop-on-powder. Binding jetting technology involves a process that makes use of two kinds of materials to create objects. These materials are a bonding agent, and a powder-based material, gypsum. The bonding agent is used to bind the powder layers together. The BJ printer functions just as a2D inkjet printer. Its nozzles extrude the binder in the form of liquid. Once a layer has been completely built, the building plate will go low to pave the way for the next layer to come on, and this procedure is repeated until the desired object under production gets to its height. The BJ 3D printing requires four materials, which are: ceramics, sand, plastics, and metals.

BJ printing does not offer high-resolution or rugged 3D products. However, it gives other advantages. One of its advantages is that it makes it possible for the designer to print an object or a part in full color. All you need to do id to add color pigments to the binder. The available color pigments include white, black, cyan, yellow, and magenta. Presently, the BJ technology has some applications for rapid prototyping and for uses in the aerospace, medical, and automotive industries. Some of the popular BJ printers include ExOne R2 and ZCorp Spectrum z510.

The Material Jetting (MJ) Polyjet and Wax Casting Technology

Material Jetting also referred to as wax casting, has a unique background. It does not have a specific inventor.

It has always been more of a technique than a 2D printing process. The Material Jetting has gained relevance among jewelers from past centuries. Wax casting is an ancient process that gives the user the opportunity to produce high-quality jewelry that us customized. The introduction of 3D printing gives it a new look, and it becomes an automated process. Presently, the MJ printers are used to make high-resolution parts that are specifically used in the dental and jewelry industries. Most jewelers presently subscribe to the MJ technology, and there are many MJ printers on the market.

The wax 3D casting printer works with the CAD file. Immediately the user uploads the CAD file to the printer; the system will start work fully. The printer makes use of its nozzle that sweeps evenly to add heated wax to the aluminum build platform in the layers that are controlled. Immediately the heated material touches the build plate; it will start to cool down and become solid. While the 3D product is build-up, there is support from a gel-like material that helps to support the process of extra complex geometries. The user can make use of his or her hand or a powerful water jet to remove the support materials after the completion of the printing. Immediately the 3D object is finally produced; it can be put to use. It does not require any further post-curing. Some MJ printers, such as Polyjet, makes use of photopolymer-resins instead of the synthetic wax. Polyjet technology produces a great resolution. Polyjet is used to create objects or parts for industries that have a wide range. Popular MJ printers include PLA 3D printer (for large format), HP Multi Jet Fusion, etc.

There is a constant growth in 3D printing technology. With this growth and new innovations, there will be a continual fall in the prices of the machines, while the printers will keep being more impressive. You need to understand that a person doesn't need to have a 3D printer to learn the technology or put it to use. This is where the business aspect of the 3D printer comes in for you if you are willing to make money from it. People who do not have a 3D printer can have access to many of the free web-based 3D printing designs which they will choose from. Once they have their designs, they will have to walk up to a person who has the 3D machine to help them print out their idea. In this instance, you stand a chance to make yourself some cool cash.

CHAPTER FOUR

INDUSTRIAL USE OF THE TECHNOLOGY DEVICE

The additive manufacturing technology has come a long way after its introduction. Although it originated as a tool for making a rapid prototype, it has, however, gained more grounds in and evolved to become relevant in many industries. The growth it enjoys has given it a place in various industries. There are lots of industrial use found for 3D printing. The method of application varies from one industry to another. However, there is a general similarity, which is tooling aids, visual and functional prototypes, and end parts. More than these uses, many companies are identifying new ways to put the 3D printing technology to use by creating new business models with the technology.

In this chapter, I will be taking you through the use of 3D printing in certain industries and across certain sectors. Many industries use it for the growth of their businesses, and it has been greatly helping them with all they seek.

The Aerospace and Defense

The expansion of the 3D printing technology into industries has the use by the aerospace and defense as a backbone. The industry and sector were among the earliest uses of the technology. They use of 3D printing by the aerospace and defense dates back to 1989, and presently, the industry has a great stake in the additive manufacturing market with 12% input. The aerospace and Defense industry keeps investing in the researches ongoing to make the 3D printing technology better than its present status. Some key players of the aerospace industry, including Airbus, Safran, Boeing, GE, and GKN are responsible largely for the growth of the additive manufacturing in aerospace and defense. The reason for their interest in 3D printing technology is its values in making: functional prototypes, tooling, and lightweight components; they are all useful to the industry.

The additive manufacturing impacts on the aerospace industry include the production of certain functional parts such as air ducts (SLS), wall panels (FDM), and structural metal components (DMLS, DED, EBM). The additive manufacturing technology is used in the aerospace and defense industry because of the following benefits:

It aids Low-volume production

3D printing is a perfect match for the quantity of production that aerospace industries demand. The aerospace industry works with the production of highly complex parts in low volume; hence, 3D printing becomes an ideal instrument in such a situation. The additive manufacturing technology makes it possible for the creation of complex geometries without the need for expensive tooling equipment. Thus, aerospace companies are able to make batches of parts at a cost-effective rate.

It supports Weight reduction

Weigh is an important factor every designer of an aircraft must put into consideration. As much as aerodynamics and engine performance are concerned, it is equally important for an aircraft to have a lightweight. When an aircraft's weight is reduced, it will reduce carbon dioxide emissions, fuel consumption, and payload. 3D printing helps to achieve all these by creating parts that are lightly weighted; hence, helping to conserve fuel.

It Gives Efficient Materials

The layering method of producing materials by the additive manufacturing machine makes it produce parts with less waste, unlike the conventional subtractive method of manufacturing. Thermoplastics, which include reinforced nylon, PAEK, etc. and metal powders, including stainless steel, titanium, aluminum, etc. are basically the 3D printed materials use for aerospace and defense parts, among others. Nevertheless, there is an increase in the availability of 3D printable materials, which is expanding, and it is giving more room for the possible application of the additive manufacturing technology in aerospace and defense.

It helps to consolidate Parts

The additive manufacturing consolidates parts by integrating multiple parts to make a single component. This helps to reduce the number of needed parts. Hence it simplifies the process of assembling and maintenance, and it reduces the time spend to assembly.

It is crucial for maintenance and repair

The additive manufacturing technology is useful for maintaining and repair of an aircraft. There are metal parts that the 3D printing technology makes, such as Direct Energy Deposition. The DED is used to repair aircraft and military equipment. Materials can also be added to worn-out surfaces of turbine blades and other high-end equipment.

The additive manufacturing is often applied in the building of aircraft engine components. As announced by the GE in 2015, the company made use of 3D printing to make a fuel nozzle for the LEAP jet engine. With the benefit of its cost efficiency and combination of complex parts, the company reached a milestone of 30,000 3D fuel nozzles in 2018. The additive manufacturing helps the company engineers to consolidate twenty distinct parts to form one part, thus, reducing the weight of the nozzle by 25%, and requiring fewer expenses to produce.

More than the engine components, 3D printing is also useful for producing parts that can be used for interior designs. 3D printed plastics are useful for interior designing of an aircraft, and there may need to replace the wall panels of an aircraft that the additive manufacturing technology is adept at making in a low-volume. The traditional manufacturing technology would make new plastic components using injection molding, which is complex and expensive for a low volume.

More into the aspect of defense, 3D printing is changing the way end parts for military equipment are made. The defense sector is making use of complex brackets and surveillance drones, as well as jet engine components and submarine hulls. With the additive manufacturing technology, engineers have the freedom to design and create a prototype of their complex circuit boards and antennas in their lab and companies without taking out the design to any third party for production, which takes time. 3D printing is great at producing antennas for electronic devices.

The additive manufacturing technology helps to make custom tooling equipment such as jigs and fixtures based on when they are demanded. Also, the 3D printer helps to make reliable and durable spare parts for the aerospace industry. One reason it is relevant in this aspect of its use is that the 3D printer gives the required parts in short lead-time. It is faster than the traditional manufacturing techniques. At the same time, more than the speed, it gives the required parts at a cost-effective rate making it possible to avoid unnecessary expenses. The aerospace and defense are crucial players among the industries utilizing 3D printing technology. The reason for this is not far-fetched, the technology offers impressive values, it improves the performance of aircraft, and provides a more agile method of producing spare parts.

The Automotive Industry

The automotive has joined the league of industries using the 3D technology for its production. The year 2018 shows a great impact on the automotive industry in the market of 3D printing with $1.4 billion worth of investments. There is an expected growth in the worth in the coming years. The 3D printing relevance is being felt in areas such as motorsports and performing racing. The 3D technology is utilized to make generative designs and topology optimization, which are making a new impact on different from the traditional approaches to part designs. At present, prototyping is the basic use of 3D printing in the automotive industry. However, the industry is making efforts to identify other possible uses, such as tooling they can put it to. There are new and innovative end-use applications for 3D printing in the automotive industry, all as a result of their relentless to find such. The additive manufacturing technology has several benefits it gives the automotive industry. Below are the benefits the industry keeps enjoying by using the 3D printer.

It helps to Develop Products faster

The development of any automotive product needs to undergo a prototype. It gives the designer the opportunity to test every part before it is produced. With 3D printing in the picture, prototyping is made easier, faster, and cheaper. The absence of tooling makes it easier for product teams to increase the pace of developing a new product.

It Creates Design Flexibility

Since designers can easily produce designs at a faster rate, they also gained greater flexibility while testing many designs. With 3D printing, designers are able to make fast changes to their designs, and they can modify in a twinkle of an eye.

Cost-Effective Customization

The additive manufacturing technology makes it less expensive for the automotive industry to make customized parts in a flexible manner. The luxury and motorsport sector of the automotive industry now adopts the 3D technology to make personalized parts for the interior and exterior of their vehicles.

It makes Complex Geometries easier

Many components of cars require complex geometries, such as the internal channels, thin walls, and fine meshes. The additive manufacturing technology makes it possible to make these complex parts in a way that they are light weighted and durable.

3D printing in the automotive industry is set on its ability to be applied to various aspects of the industry activities. Tooling aids are essential factors in the production of a high-quality part. The additive manufacturing technologies, including FDM, and SLS, have been helpful in making tooling aids at a relatively low price, which is presently helping the automotive industry perform at its capacity. With 3D printing, it is impressively lower in cost to customize a tooling aid than it is with the traditional manufacturing method.

Ford is one of the automotive companies that has successfully utilized 3D printing to make tooling. It was awarded in 2018 as a means of recognition.

Also, 3D printing in the automotive industry has helped with prototyping making. It gives the possibility to produce design iterations in multiples within a short period of time. Consistent improvement in the technology has made it become effective at producing functional prototypes via the use of high-end materials such as ULTEM, and PEEK. Similarly, to the production of spare parts in the aerospace industry, the additive manufacturing technology also helps with the production of spare parts for the automotive. It impacts the production of spare parts by making it available on demand. Parts are being produced locally, whenever they are needed. The result of this is that the company spends less on inventory, and it takes lesser time to have whatever part is needed.

However, a critical disadvantage of the use of 3D printing in the automotive industry is the high volume of parts that the industry needs to produce from time to time. The industry produces over 100,000 parts annually. Nonetheless, there have been impressive improvements in the rate at which printers work, and their sizes have increased to aid them to work effectively. Hence, additive manufacturing technology is fast becoming viable for a medium-size production volume, especially in the automotive sector that deals with motorsport and luxury vehicles, which produces a lower volume of vehicles. Even BMW is deeply delving into the use of 3D printing. It had a production of over 1 million 3D parts in the last ten years. The additive manufacturing technology is fast changing the methods and ways vehicles are being produced in recent times. The primary reason for the relevance of 3D printing in the automotive industry is its ability to fasten the process of producing parts and at the same time, reduce the price of production.

Medicine and Dentistry

The tentacles of 3D printing have been extended to the field of medicine and dentistry. More than 90% of the medical Additive manufacturing professionals are assured that 3D printing will keep being relevant in the industry. The additive manufacturing is serving the medical industry in the area of prosthetics, and bioprinting, among others. 3D printing technology offers medical practitioners the ability to provide personalized patient care at a friendly cost. Also, in the use of CT, 3D printing helps to provide solutions to some patient's health challenges. Including implants and dental appliances. There are quite lots of benefits that 3D printing affords the medical field.

It helps to optimize medical devices

The additive manufacturing technology makes it easier to optimize or create designs for medical devices. With its low-cost of prototyping, it has become easier for medical practitioners to develop new designs for new devices, and this helps to make more medical devices that are effectively available at the market.

It makes Personalized Healthcare easier and accessible

The 3D printer has the capacity to make patient-specific devices. This ability is what the medical industry is utilizing to make more of such devices. It is easier and faster to produce devices such as prosthetics and implants at a relatively low price, unlike conventional manufacturing technology.

The additive manufacturing has a large variant of applications in the medical and dental industry. Among its application, it finds relevance more in the production of hearing aids. According to reports, more than 5% of the world population is experiencing hearing disability, and going by the World Health Organization's report (WHO), the percentage will rise to 10% by 2050. Hence, a well-informed businessman will foresee a wider market for hearing aids in the coming future, in which

3D printing is a form of an answer. There are over 90% hearing aids produced from the 3D technology, and more will still be produced. The SLA is used when the production of hearing aids is involved. Its choice is based on the fact that it is highly detailed and has dimensional accuracy for parts that are small. With this, a custom-fit hearing aid can be produced.

Just as it is making a wave in the general medicine industry, the additive manufacturing technology is also showing is relevance in digital dentistry. The introduction of digitalization into the dental sector is fast improving the result dentists get in their services. 3D scanners and materials are more accessible today, and they are taking the place of traditional means of creating dental impressions. When 3D printing is fused with intraoral scanning, dental products such as bridges, bite splints, and crowns that will match the anatomy of a patient are perfectly produced. 3D printing helps with the dental implantology success rate; this helps with the accuracy and quality of works done in dentistry. Surgical devices and guides are produced faster and at a cheap rate.

According to Formlabs, a company that manufactures SLA and SLS report that the machines have helped with the production of a surgical guide that has aided over 50,000 surgeries. The additive manufacturing technology makes use of biocompatible plastic or metal, such as titanium materials to make custom prosthetic and orthopedic devices.

The additive manufacturing technology is not developed to the extent that it will produce a 3D printed body part. However, it can make artificial living tissues that will reflect natural tissue features. The processes of making the artificial tissue feature is what is we called *Bioprinting*. Bioprinting is a technology used for research study and testing. It has impressive potential in the field of regenerative medicine. In bioprinting, the 3D printer is considered a bioprinter, and the bioprinter set living cells in layers, the result is called bio-link, and they mimic real organ tissues. The bio-link is used in place of plastics and metals. Other structures such as cartilage, skin, blood vessels, cardiac patches, and bone are also fabricated with 3D bioprinting.

The use of the additive manufacturing technology in the medical and dental industry is increasing as hospitals are now utilizing the 3D printer in their labs to produce anatomy models that are specific to their patients. The patient's MRI and CT scans determine the method the 3D printer will take to create the anatomy models using some 3D printer materials such as Material jetting to make sure that the models retain precision and originality. The models are made available for surgeons to plan and practice for surgery before the actual surgery. The method has helped to fasten procedures, improve the precision level of surgery, and reduce the possibility of invasion. The medical and dental industry accounts for 11% of the overall market of 3D printing. Its relevance in the industry lies in the production of personalized healthcare, an improvement in presurgical preparation, and the innovation in the drive device.

For Consumer Goods

The need to stay relevant in a competitive market has made the consumer-oriented industries search for possible means of adapting to the demands of their consumers. One way is the use of 3D printing technology. Additive manufacturing helps many consumer goods-producing companies to meet the needs of their consumers by offering a cost-effective approach to the development of products; it's testing and eventual production. Many companies involved in the production of toys, sport wears, and electronics in the industry are embracing 3D printing technology. With the increase in the availability of 3D printers, many designers and engineers are gaining access to it, and this is resulting in more development in the production of goods. The additive manufacturing technology benefits to the consumer goods-producing industry are enormous.

It improves the standard of product

With 3D printing, it has become easier to test and validate a product before it is actually produced to know its durability and quality. 3D printing helps with a faster means of producing prototypes and models of products at a relatively low price. The results from the study carried out on a model is what will help to know how and where to improve on a product before it is finally produced.

Increase the time of Production and Availability of the product

More products tend to be available at the market faster than before with the introduction of 3D printing into the manufacturing industry. Once a product is developed faster, the next step is to produce it and take it to the market.

It offers mass customization of products

3D printing offers service in the area of personalized products to suit the taste of consumers. The traditional method of production is only cost-effective when it involves mass production; however, for low production, it is quite expensive. However, 3D printing is cost-effective in the production of products, and it makes it easier to customize products based on the requirements of the customers. This is an advantage that many companies are making use of to stay afloat in the market.

Additive manufacturing technology helps to improve the standard of products. For example, Adidas, a footwear company, made use of 3D printing to make midsoles for one of its products – Futurecraft. The midsoles have some materials that make the product perform well for various sports activities. The midsole is designed with 20,000 struts that give it an impressive cushioning. The traditional method cannot create this, not even the injection or the compression molding techniques.

The cosmetics and beauty sector is also enjoying the impact of 3D printing on its activities. In 2018, the popular French fashion company – Chanel introduced the first 3D printed mascara brush. SLS technology was utilized in the process of making the brush. The additive manufacturing technology has improved the standard of the brush. There is a strong adhesion between mascara and lashes as a result of the optimization of the rough and granular texture of the brush. The success of Chanel was the breakthrough in 3D printing in the cosmetic sector. Nonetheless, it has proven that additive manufacturing technology can impact cosmetic products, hence the possible need for it in the future.

For Industrial Goods

Industrial goods are machines, and machinery parts, tooling as well as other equipment that are utilized to make products. Many companies in the production of the machines are constantly making efforts to beat down the cost of production, and this has made them opt for the additive manufacturing technology in their process of producing the high-end machines. 3D printing technology helps the industry to stay innovative, agile, and responsive. 3D printing usefulness in the industrial good is enumerated below.

It helps with complex designs

As noted in other industrial productions, prototypes are crucial. Similarly, 3D printing is utilized in making a prototype for industrial goods under production. When there are complexities, such as the need to modify a specific design, rather than waiting for weeks, or a long number of days that the traditional manufacturing technology offers, 3D printing has made it faster, and such design would be ready in a week.

It Reduces Lead time

One other benefit of 3D printing is that it helps to reduce lead times, and this is why more than 50% of companies in the production of industrial goods embrace it. There is no need for tooling; this helps to reduce the time requires for the production of parts. And it makes it possible to bypass the tooling process, which is time-consuming and expensive.

Immediate availability of goods

The additive manufacturing method uses a digital file, which is uploaded to the printer to make a product. This process makes it faster to have a product ready in a couple of hours. This makes it possible for companies to rely on it to provide goods on demand.

The additive manufacturing technology has been applied in the making of end-use parts. An instance is its use in the transformation of the production of bearings, at Bowman Additive Production. Bowman was able to produce its Rollertrain cage using HP's Multi Jet Fusion and PA11 nylon material. Also, 3D printing helps in the production of tooling. The use of additive manufacturing technology for the production of manufacturing aids such as gauges, jigs, and fixtures makes it gain approval from the industrial goods manufacturing companies. 3D printing technology is used to transform the making of certain hard tooling such as molds. Molds are used for injection molding and die casting. Using the traditional method, making molds involved CNC mills, and it involves multiple design iterations. It often takes weeks, and at times, months for the original design desired to be finished. There is a representation of time-wasting, high expenses, and wastage of materials.

However, additive manufacturing technology such as SLM and DMLS, can be utilized to make the tooling. It saves cost, increases the time of production, and also enhances the functionality of the mold. An example of companies embracing 3D printing technology is Eckhart. Eckhart recently embraced the additive manufacturing technology to replace existing metal tools with the tools produced by the 3D printer. 3D printing provides new methods of manufacturing and doing business to arrive at a better innovation.

CHAPTER FIVE

MATERIALS AND OTHER COMPONENTS

Additive manufacturing technology works with numerous materials in the process of producing products. Unlike the traditional method of production that is limited to a few plastics of less value, 3D printing offers an abundance of materials. The growth in the additive manufacturing technique has paved the way for more materials such as steel, carbon fiber, nylon, and many other advanced materials to function. Notwithstanding the material involved, the 3D printing method is a better option than the traditional method because it makes geometry production faster and easier. The availability of many materials for 3D printing makes it quite hard to make a decision on which material to use for a specific production. For every part, you want to make, either a prototype, end-use product, or a tool, you need to select the best and right material. 3D printing has three common materials – Plastics, metals, and composites. Among these three, plastic takes the lead in popularity. However, metal and composite are also gaining grounds, and they combine the automatic working of 3D printing with high-performance materials.

The Plastic Materials for 3D printing

The plastic 3D printing is well developed than every other form of 3D printing, and it has a wide range of materials that can be utilized for production. The materials used for plastic 3D printing include polypropylene, ABS, Nylon, and polyetherimide, which is a high-temperature plastic. For the plastic 3D printing, most of its materials require curing and post-processing. Nonetheless, there is still a reduction in lead time up to weeks, unlike the traditional method of fabrication. Below are the plastic materials:

Polypropylene (PP): This material is cheap, has the capacity to make up living hinges, and it resists chemicals. However, it is flammable and has a degradation status with UV light. PP is used in the making of lab equipment, household materials, and textiles.

Acrylonitrile butadiene styrene (ABS): it is the most popular among the plastic 3D printing materials, and it is generally acceptable. For a beautifying production, the ABS is perfect. Mechanical properties made with ABS enjoy aesthetic and a well-balanced spread. ABS is often used for toys, telephones, kitchen utensils, and other daily products.

Nylon: it is rigid, durable, and strong. However, nylon is quite costly, and it does not resist strong acids and bases. Applications that need high mechanical properties and components that are considered under-the-hood are the products it is basically used for.

Polyetherimide (PEI): this material is used for designs that can withstand high intense heat. It is very expensive, but it is great for making injection mold tools and components that resist heat.

The Metal Materials for 3D printing

Metal has been experiencing hype among designers who make use of it make products and parts. 3D technologies such as selective laser melting (SLM), and direct metal laser sintering (DMLS) have contributed to the influx of metal as materials used in 3D printing. The materials of metal include titanium, stainless steel, and aluminum are great for their strength and durability. 3D printing is the technology that is suitable for producing materials. Metal materials require post-processing. However, it does not require much labor like the traditional method.

Stainless steel: it is a very common material in most industries. Architecture, medicine, among others, are the industries utilizing it. Kitchen utensils, car parts, and surgical instruments are beneficiaries of its functionality. Stainless steel is durable and versatile. 3D printing makes it easier and cheaper to produce. Hence, it takes away the need for manual labor and makes production possible automatically and faster.

Aluminum: this is a malleable and lightweight material. It is popular among metal materials. Aluminum is used in food packaging, airplanes, laptops, among others. The traditional machining has been relegated with the use of 3D printing for a lot of aluminum applications.

Titanium: it is the strongest among all the metallic materials, and the most expensive. It is made up of fatigue resistant, very hard and tough, and it is biocompatible. The material has a wide range of benefits. However, the cost serves as a limitation that makes it useful for a few productions such as surgical implants and high-end automotive parts or components.

The Composite Materials for 3D Printing

There have been many composite parts in the market following the successful use of composite materials in 3d printing. Composite materials are composed of a matrix, including a polymer, and a reinforcement, like carbon fiber. When composite materials are used, the object will have an improved mechanical property that is above that of the traditional methods and materials. The traditional method was slow and tedious in the process (which was a lay-up fabrication process). However, composite 3D printing has dealt with the lengthy time frame of production, and a designer can easily finish the process of production in hours rather than weeks.

Carbon fiber: this is stronger than any metallic material when the strength-to-weight ratio is considered. It is a material that helps to make objects that are strong, more lightweight, and stiffer. It gives bikes, cars, and aircraft their efficiency and speed.

Fiberglass: This is a composite material that gives the basic benefits that composite 3D printing to offer at a cheap rate. Fiberglass gives a strong stiffness-to-weight ratio to wind turbines, boat hulls, and circuit boards. It is can perform for many purposes, and very cost-effective. The material makes it easy to access high performance in different industries.

3D printing keeps enjoying growth as the year goes by. The continual growth is shifting the focus of 3D printing from consumer-oriented only to professional and industrial uses. The use of 3D printing to create prototypes, end-use products, and tools in different industries is a show of the shift in its use. All new innovations and expansion of 3D printing are primarily geared toward saving them time and money for engineers and designers.

CHAPTER SIX

STARTING A BUSINESS WITH TECHNOLOGY

You are welcome to the second part of this guide. I am welcoming you because it is the part that will dwell on how well you can make money from all you have learned in the first part of the book. In the previous part, I mentioned the uses of 3D printing in certain industries and how it benefits those industries. The knowledge of those benefits is what will serve as empirical proof that 3D printing has come to stay, and it is worthy of your time, commitment, and possibly investment. Every one of those benefits is what will always drive the industries always to want to have the 3D printing technology and its services. To build your 3D printing, there are certain things you need to put in place. It will determine the future of your business, and whether it will stand the test of time or not. I have identified nine steps for you to take to make your 3D printing business success.

Draw a Business Plan

For every business to be successful, the business needs a business plan. The business plan is what reveals what your business stands for, its ideals, the functions or services it has set out to render, and the discovery of certain things you do not know. One crucial element of a business plan is that it must be clear and not vague. In your business plan, you need to consider answering the following questions:

What will be the cost of the startup and later running of the business?

Who is the business target market?

How long will it take the business to break even?

What name will the business have?

To make it easier for you, I have research done on each of these questions for you.

The Startup cost

Setting up a 3D printing business does not require a huge amount. It is at a minimal rate. You may start with your home, not necessarily opening an office. Hence, you would have skipped the need to pay for lease, nor anyone to pay for being a staff. You can get your 3D printer by going for a commercial model with $6000 or possibly less. The price of the printer is the highest expense you have to deal with as you start the business. You may have to create awareness for your business by either creating a professional website, which will cost you around $500 to advertise your services. You may also advertise your service online, which will lead to a budget of around $2000 or less.

The Running expenses

The 3D printing business does not have a huge amount of expenses while the business is running. Since you are based at home, you will only have an expense that covers paying to host your website, which goes for less than $100 annually. If you wish, you may end the advertisement cost. Aside from all of these, the only cost left is to keep re-stocking materials that will aid you to print whenever you have jobs to do.

Who the target market is

The 3D printing business tends to give you the different choices of clients based on the aspect of printing you want to engage yourself in. You may be interested in hobbyists. Hobbyists have selected groups of people with a very strong interest and the financial buoyancy to carry out their interests. Some of them are collectors, and all they probably want from you is to replace parts for the model train they have, while some are gamers, who are interested in printing objects for their campaigns, and roles.

How you can make money in the 3D printing business

If you are into the 3D printing business, you will make your money by simply printing and delivering 3D models of objects, parts, or shapes to people. You can also make money by designing for customers who find it difficult to print their desired shapes in any other place.

How much you can charge your customers

The charges you are giving customers will vary based on different factors, such as the size of the product, the complexity involved in its production, and the type of materials that you use to make the product or design. If what you are designing and printing is a small item such as a miniature shopping cart, you can go for as low as $4, while a larger and more complex product, such as a terrain, used in a tabletop war game may incur up to $200 or above in charges. Your charges will be determined by the niche of the item.

How much you can make in 3D printing Business

No one can say of the specific amount you can make in the 3D printing business. According to a report by a research company, a 3D designer and printer make an average of $53,000 annually, however. The report was done by focusing on designers that print for corporations, and not themselves. Nonetheless, you will still make your profit, just like every other specialty shop. You will make more money if you have access to the best combo of various products, niche market, and needed advert.

How you can make your business more profitable

To make your business become more profitable, you need to make it visible to others. When people know your business more, it will get their attention and increase your chance of making more money. Making your business visible involves you to write for blogs as a guest. When your audience reads your blogs, they will become intimated on what you do. You may also offer to print what your community needs, such as prosthetics, to create a very good relationship and become known. You can also give out 3D printed products as a gift to people around you. I will talk more about this in a later chapter.

What name to give your business

You need to use the right name for your business. The name you choose will be what others will refer you with. It is best if you identify whether the name you are choosing has not been used by any other person before on the website and make use of it before another person comes up with the idea. Once you have your name set, immediately create a domain for your business by registering a domain name for it. Create a professional email account that will carry your business name, and you are set to go.

Make your Business a Legal Entity

A wise move is to make your business a legal entity that is dependent on you. When your business becomes a legal entity, such as an LLC, you would be prevented from facing charges personally whenever your business is sued. To make your business legal, you can choose from different structures such as corporations, LLC, and DBA. Have your privacy protected, and stay compliant by utilizing the service of a registered agent. If your business is just starting, it is often best to go for the LLC option.

Register your Business for Taxes

To set up your business, you need to have your business registered for both federal and state taxes. All you need to do is to apply for an EIN, which is quite easy and free to do. The IRS website offers the EIN for free, through fax, or mail. The EIN refers to Employer Identification Number, and it is also called the Federal Employer Identification Number. The EIN is a special number that the IRS, which is the Internal Revenue Service assigns to businesses that are operating in the US, as a means of identification. The numbers are specifically used for administering taxes and no other thing.

Set up a Business Bank Account and Credit card

A business banking and credit account are important to protect your personal assets. You need to avoid mixing your properties with the business asset. When you mix them together, your property may suffer when your business is sued. The advice here is for you to pierce your corporate veil. When you open a separate account for your business, you would have saved your personal asset and have an easy means of carrying out your accounting and tax filing.

The business credit card will make it possible for you to separate your personal expenses from your business expenses. Your company will easily create a credit history of its own, which will work out later to benefit your company when there is a need to borrow for investment.

Create a Business Accounting

There should be a well-documented account of your expenses and your income. When you are able to trace the source f your income, and the destination of your spending, you will understand how your business performs financially. Also, with a detailed account of your business, it will be easier for you to do your annual tax filing.

Obtain the Needed Licenses and Permits

A colossal mistake a person can make in the 3D printing and design business is to start without a license and other permits. If such a person is favored, he or she may have to pay fine. However, the business can be shut down on a bad day. There are specific permits and license to get.

License from the State

Depending on your state, some state permits may be needed for you to run your 3D business. To know whether it is applicable in your state, you may visit SBA's reference on state licenses and permits. It is a requirement for every business to receive sales tax on every product sold or service rendered.

Get a trademark and copyright protection

For any new product you want to develop, or new idea, concept, and design, you should endeavor to protect your right to such product to avoid plagiarism and imitation. All need to do to protect it is to register for the right trademarks and copyrights.

Ensure Your Business

Insurance is on the list of what you must do to get your 3D printing business started. In some states, worker's compensation insurance is a basic requirement; hence, if that is the state in your state, you need to go for it.

Make a Definition for your Brand

The brand you create is what your business represents and how you would like people, including your prospective buyers, to see and understand your business. Hence, it must be well done in order to avoid passing across the wrong information, or people misinterpreting your business ideals. When you give your business a great brand, it will protect it from competitors. Branding your business involves promoting it and keeping your customers glued to your services.

Promoting your 3D Printing Business

One way to make your brand known is to advertise your business using a professional website. Social media is also a great platform for you to reach more people than you can ever think of. On social media platforms, such as Instagram, you may post pictures of your previous works, and through Facebook, you can advertise your business by paying for professional advertisements.

Keeping the Customers coming

It is a different thing to have a lot of people know about your business and have them come immediately. However, it is another thing entirely for those set of people to come back for their future productions. When you have more customers coming back for your services, your business has recorded a great success for making more converts. The advertisement you are paying for, the articles you write are not just to make people see what you do, but to make them come for it and keep coming afterward

Create a Strong Web Presence

Creating a strong web presence will make your business become more visible. You can create a website where customers and prospective customers can easily visit to learn about your products and services. The goal is to make your brand known to as many people as possible.

Aside from these steps listed above, you may be wondering whether you are making the right choice by going into the 3D printing business. The possible question I have ear people ask themselves is:

Is this the right business for me?

Well, whether the business is best for you, particularly, I cannot say categorically. However, I can say that this business is quite okay for artists, especially an artist that has done some statues and carving previously. The essential part of the 3D printing job is the ability to make use of a great idea to form a physical object by fusing software and certain artistic skills.

Other questions are:

What does the 3D printing business involve?

The activities that go on in a 3D printing business are designing new 3D products, and getting them to the customers to sell. The printing process is what constitutes most of the time in the 3D printing business, and after this, you will have to spend more time on ways to advertise your business using social media and web platforms.

What experience and skills do I need to build a successful 3D printing business?

Making 3D designs require software, such as Blender, and the skill of how it works. If you are the one d=carrying out the design personally, then you need to understand how to operate the 3D printer and troubleshoot it. Lastly, you have to familiarize yourself with the 3D printing market so you can make well-informed decisions on how to approach the market with your products.

What growth potential does a D printing have?

This is one question a person tends to ask to be sure of the future of the business. However, you do not need to panic. 3D printing is not a fad; neither is it fading out. It has a large potential growth. The market has been estimated to keep growing.

As you start your 3D printing business, there is one last thing I will say, which is you getting a business mentor. Getting quality mentorship on business will guide in your decisions and prevent errors. There are free business resources around you. Just link up with one of them to acquire the help you actually need. As a startup, the mentor will serve as a support network that you can turn to when you are faced with challenges.

Solve a Problem

You don't just start a business. There must be something unique you are doing in the business. As mentioned earlier, you need to identify a niche to make an optimal profit. When you think of setting your brand, you need to seek out the needs of your customers or prospective customers. If your interest is in women, what do you want to design for them? Will they really go for it? Why would they go for it? Once you have arrived at a conclusion, start working in line with it, and make sure you become better at it.

Know when to Collaborate

In most cases, the 3D printing business is done by a person. However, since most of the work is done from your home, you may have to collaborate with other designers to maximize the number of shapes or products you sell.

CHAPTER SEVEN

MAKING YOUR BUSINESS KNOWN

A known business is a growing business. When your3D printing business gets the approval of others and gains a commonplace in the minds of many people, it will start yielding great rewards. As much as there is a market for 3D printing, you are required, however, to make extra effort to make sure that the business is well developed to arrive at the vision you have for the business. It is not easy to make money from 3D printing. However, it is not unattainable. This is the joy of it. The more ground your business covers, the more profits you tend to make from it. I have studied the ideas of professionals, entrepreneurs, and potential clients who have impacts on the 3D printing market. From my study, I have identified useful ideas you can use to expand and grow your business. Nonetheless, you need to understand that these ideas are not magic. Hence, you do not expect everything to work instantly. They require time and space to help take your vision for the business to the height you want. You always need to remember that for every business, there is competition, and this is one factor you have to stay ahead to achieve your target. With hard work, persistence, and consistency, you will utilize these ideas to your great benefits and see awesome results.

Get Started at the Right Time

One great mistake many people make when they go into a business is to rush into it, by allowing the factors surrounding the business, such as competition, be their motivation. Many people who do this are most often than not, not prepared for the business. They either lack the basic skills needed to get started rightly or do not have the capacity to face the requirement of the business at the point. Hence, it is important for you to get started when it is right. As a startup, you don't necessarily have to give your present job. It is not necessary to leave school. Actually, you need to keep your job as it will help you to build your business. Also, your schooling should continue. You should even strive to have a degree in engineering or design, and also probably get a minor in Business. All these are what will build you for the tasks ahead.

The advice is you should never rush yourself into the business. Getting more experienced will help you start the business in an established manner, and it will be easier for you at this point to start building your credibility and contact. Every magnificent building you see out there stands on a solid and durable foundation. When you place your business on a strong foundation, it would have developed the fortitude to withstand any storm that may come against it.

Avoid Obscurity and Be Visibly Active

To build your company, you need to make it known to others. The process of making it known involves your active participation on platforms that will bring you and your business to the limelight. You need to make new friends, create records of activeness on media forums such as Facebook groups, or 3D Hubs talk. There is also the 3D printing Reddit and many more platforms for you to make yourself known by being a participant. Your potential clients are on these platforms, but they won't know about you if they don't hear from you, either directly when you talk, or indirectly when others you have worked with tell them. As you make comments and create posts, be nice, and create a good name for yourself on those platforms. Your name on the platform may end up becoming your brand for your 3D printing business, and if you have created a wrong impression with them, they will likely turn your haters, not clients.

While you are on the platforms, it is not enough for you to comment, or share knowledge with others. People love seeing to believe; thus, you need to make them see your worth by posting your past works. Let them have a taste of your designs, your prototypes, and models. Instagram is a great social media you can utilize to display the pictures of your works. You may also use YouTube by creating videos of your works; trying to edit them will be great to make your business soar. All you have to do is bring all your social networks together. The more views, comments, likes, and messages you get, the more visible your business is becoming. While you share your works, try to share some of them for free; when it is free, many people will access them and produce them for their use. This way, they will have a feel of your work's quality and come back for more, which they will have to pay for. The idea is to build trust, and that you have achieved. While you share your designs for free, you need to protect it from someone who may want to resell it. Protect it by having it on popular 3D printing file libraries as soon as possible, and adding watermarks to it.

Don't be One-Sided

In the 3D printing business, you need to avoid being one-sided in your service. Basically, 3D printing involves the design and printing aspects. The design has proven to be more profitable anyways. This is because many customers want their products designed and printed altogether. Only in a few instances do we have customers coming with a model or design that they need to print. Hence, to build your business and make it grow as wish, you should be available to render the needed service of both designing and printing. Many customers at the consumer level do not come back. When you major in printing, having large prints that come with high profits will make your business grow; however, many of the printing jobs don't come alone. Hence, the business will end up experiencing many small, low-profit prints.

Printing takes time and resources, and it may deter you from being able to maintain your business for growth. Hence, paying attention to deigning will be a better option. With designs, your business will make more money than taking prints on demand. Therefore, in your 3D printing business, you need to treat every customer the same way. Also, make sure you set a fair price, and it is appropriate. Customers want a person that can solve all of their problems, and if not all, most of the problems. Be a problem solver. The basic problem of your customers in the 3D printing industry is to have an object that is designed from scratch and printed. Make yourself available for this, and you will always rank first among their choices. To make your business grow, you need to go beyond just 3D printing services, but also offer services in designs.

Identify your Niche

As you start with various jobs, designs, models, and printing, you should be on the lookout for an aspect or a niche you are good at. At times, your area of specialty may not be what you have in mind. You may stumble on it by accident. However, paying attention to it more will give you a strength you can always rely on to make a name for yourself in the 3D printing business. It is possible for you to have your strength in items you do not plan to sell. However, looking for a way to make it the business will help you make more. Also, as you engage in more printing, you will be learning more with every new project that comes your way. So, pay attention to every new project you do and check out their possible relevancies in the market. You can start thinking of new jigs, gadgets, and fixtures you can possibly design and sell to companies that require them. Identifying your niche will create a space for you and give you a specific branding that will make you become more visible to others and prospective customers.

Use the Best Tools for your Projects

As you make new prints for your clients, you need to give them quality output. Your product's quality is highly determined by the machine you make use of to make it, aside from your skills. So, you need to get efficient tools that will make your products come out fine as you and the clients have desired. There are ready-to-use desktop machines, and these are what most professionals and companies use; however, there are specific 3D printers that are built for the purpose of open source DIY designs. You need to identify the one you need for your niche and obtain it. For example, if your niche is surrounding the printing of pendants or necklace pieces, you should do research and study on a suitable printer for the production.

If your interest is in 3D printing using plastic materials, there are printers that will adequately suit your need; such is the ZMorph 2.0 SX Basic Set. It is suitable because it has in-built closed-loop functionality. However, if your interest is in various materials for your models and prototypes, you may use the ZMorph 2.0 SX Full Set. It has the capacity to print 3D that is cut with a CNC tool head and has an engraving done with a laser.

Make Use of 3D Hubs

In the process of building your 3D printing business, never forget to utilize the 3D Hubs as a means to achieve your aim. 3D hubs are notable for being the biggest platform where people order custom 3D prints form providers. Also, there are many professionals on the platform seeking high-quality prints from providers that are reliable. As you make use of the platform, your target should encompass both the custom service seekers and the professionals who want high-quality products. The professionals often seek partners from the local providers, and this promises to give your business long term opportunity of making money.

3D Hubs is a created specifically for 3D printing business, and there is a high level of competition on the platform, hence to be ahead and make your business grow, you need some tips.

Make sure your profile is impressive (make it visual) for you to get orders. You should start with a low price tag and increase them as you make a wave on the platform.

Always work well to get good reviews from clients. The reviews are what will draw more customers to you.

If you are just starting, on the 3D Hubs, it is advisable you start with printing on demand first, and then build your customer base with that.

You should give out promo materials alongside your orders so that the clients you work for will remember you, and this will also serve as a way of advertising your business.

Identify your niche, which may be in engineering, architecture, or design for customers, etc.

Make use of social media to connect with your clients; among the social media platform to use, Facebook, LinkedIn are awesome, and you may also use the 3D Hubs Talk for community and advice.

To promote your business, Instagram is another wonderful choice you can go for always. All you need to do is identify relevant people you can follow and share your works with them.

You can also feature the stories of your projects on a local 3D printing media.

One thing you need to know, however, is that there is no specific rule on how to be successful as a 3D printing business person. There are different factors, such as time, place, and people that determine how things work. At times, you need to work in line with the circumstances if you must get the desired result. You need to be open-minded and flexible in your decisions, making the process.

CHAPTER EIGHT

WHAT TO HAVE FOR THE BUSINESS

3D printing is fast becoming an area of interest for many people. Hence, it has become the winning way for everyone who wishes to make a fortune in our ever-developing world of technology. To kick start the 3D printing, there are certain items you need to gather. I will take you through these items in this chapter.

The 3D printer

Of course, the 3D printer is an important item you need to get to embark on any project you want to do. When you come up with sketches for different items such as customized eyewear, a robot prototype, customized toy, the 3D printer is what you need to make all these become a physical object that you can hold.

The 3D printer is the basic equipment you need make use of your technical skills, and add your artistic skills to make money. The 3D printer is quite accessible, and this has spelled out its uniqueness, among many other technologies that are used for manufacturing. At the same time, since it is accessible, many people who desire to make objects out of their ideas can now see their dreams coming to realization. The 3D printer produces objects and their parts, the tools to work, and artistic works also.

You may decide to outsource your creations to a third-party for printing as a starter. To do that, you only need to get a 3D printing vendor. It is always cool if you can get an in-house printer. To print form a third party, or get yourself a 3D printer, there are certain questions you need to provide answers to. The answers will help you to make the right choice on the 3D printer you are getting for your business and possibly on the right person to give the project you have to. The following are the questions you should ask in your bid to go for the 3D printer:

What is my expected volume of print runs?

Carrying out 3D production is time-consuming. Hence, if your target is to make a high volume of designs and printing, with interest in printing at a faster rate, you need to look for 3D printers that are designed with fast processing speed. You will have to locate a third party that has a fast printer also if you are outsourcing your production.

What Scale will the object, which I desire have?

The size of the object you want to produce also matters. For objects with small sizes, you can get an entry-level fused deposition manufacturing printer (FDM). FDM produces objects with 4" around. However, if your objects are larger sizes, you will have to opt for a high-end filament printer that has the capacity for objects with 10"x 6" x 6" size.

Which materials will I be using primarily in the course of my productions?

Some printers are useful for making objects with materials other than plastics. Your choice of materials needs to be a factor that will determine your choice of the printer to buy.

What level of detail will my products have?

Printers come in different capacities for detail creations for each design. Most printers are capable of making objects with minimal details; however, if your interest is in a detailed high-level production, then you may have to select your printer carefully. A stereolithographic printer (SL) will work effectively. The printed objects from the SL are of high resolution, and they are produced with the use of photosensitive resin and UV laser.

Software

Software is the next properties of the 3D printing business you must have at your fingertip if you want to go into the business. There is a lot of software out there. Some are free open-source. You may also get some online for your products as a starter. However, as much as you grow, you need to start opting for other 3D modeling software that is packaged with 3D printing features. The software is accessible following a year's license subscription. There are specific 3D workflow modeling tools you must identify in any software choice you plan to make. You should look out for the printer models for 3D output, look if it has the ability to orient models appropriately on the print bed, and check if it supports generation, this is what makes sure that the models are always stable in the process of printing.

Thermoplastic Filament

The next important item you need is the materials for printing your models. You should carefully think about certain features you want to see in the products you make. Look at the durability, strength, and precision level of the products. The materials you want will most definitely be one that is sturdy, universal, and works well with your printer. The thermoplastic filament is often used by many professionals, engineers, and designers. The polylactic acid is one of the most used type of the thermoplastic filament, while the acrylonitrile butadiene styrene (ABS) is the second most popular type. There are different color shades of the filament in spools, and usually, it comes with 1.75mm or 3mm thickness. From a spool, one can get up to 400 pieces of chess.

Sampling Kit for Materials

There are sampling kits you can lay your hands on. They will help you make the right decisions on which material to use for building a specific object. The purpose of the sampling kits is to help you test the materials before you start making use of them. Your 3D objects can also come from sandstone, metals, and ceramics, aside from thermoplastic. However, when you use non-plastic material to print, you may get a mixed result. This is because using non-plastic materials is a form of experimental printing.

Invest in Personal Training

This may sound unnecessary or tautological. However, I wouldn't want to leave any stone unturned. You need to invest in yourself by engaging in training that will make you become a better person. you can take a course on animation. You may learn it online, and there are visual effects technology school you can also enroll in to learn. Always look for ways to improve yourself. The idea is to have *Knowledge*. Knowledge is the last tool or property you need to make your 3D printing business a successful venture. You cannot afford to have many loopholes when it comes to 3D printing as someone who has an investment in it. You can improve yourself on modeling, and probably texture. By increasing your knowledge, your business will be placed on a great platform for growth.

CHAPTER NINE

DEALING WITH GENERAL BUSINESS CHALLENGES

Running a business is not an easy task. You need to be hard working, and make sure you update it. The rate at which economy and technology are evolving in our world today is a clear explication of the truth that what may seem to work yesterday is obviously useless today. Hence, to stay on top of the game, one needs to always be on the alert. The ability to solve the challenge is what makes a distinction between the growing businesses and the struggling ones. In your bid to make money from 3D printing, an unfortunate mistake you may make is thinking the 3D printing is not like every other business. Just like every other business that produces goods and renders services have customers that receive their products and services, you also in the 3D printing business have customers that receive your designs, and final 3D printed objects. Hence, you need to be on the lookout for possible challenges that may hinder the progress of your company. I have identified eight possible challenges your business may face, and I will give you the answer to each of these challenges.

Gradual Fading of Integrity

The moral challenge is one of the major issues facing many businesses today. Every business owner wants to be richer; the staff wants the promotion, more commission, and to stay at their jobs. Even some business owners are ready to give bribes as long as the contract will be theirs. There is the urge to cut corners in order to ahead. The result of this is that many people begin to resort to lying and gradually graduate to stealing from the business, which will eventually dive the nose of the company into a great sea of destruction. What integrity degradation does to a business is that it builds distrust between the employers and the employees, the executives and shareholders, or even between partners. When a business lacks integrity and trust, it is obviously suffering from internal strife, and that will hinder it from being able to perform actions in the competitive market out there. You need to make sure that the environment of your business is filled with trust and integrity. Make your customers Have trust in you, and you will be amazed at how much your business would grow.

Financial Management

One other area of challenge for most business is finance. Finance is important in the running of any business. It is great to make high profits; however, how are you spending the profits? If your business has a capital expenditure or receivable collections that are more than your profits, your business is like a ship that is about to sink. Financial management involves you being able to pay attention to the generation of the cash flow. To deal with financial management challenges, you need to capitalize on your business appropriately, and you should set up a cash reserve to deal with every obligations or emergency whenever they arise. As a business owner, you need to know when you need to be more prudent financially in the course of running your business. As a starter, you may be in charge of your financial accounting. However, it is also better for you to employ the skill of a professional.

Increase in Competition

Setting up a business is no longer tedious as it was in the past. Once you get yourself a domain name and register your business, you already have a business. However, making your business stay and grow is more demanding. It is where the challenge is for most people. This I why we have many startups, but fewer existing businesses. The challenge is how to compete with the various strong companies in the market before you and after you. However, it is fortunate that there are more experts online. You can ask these experts questions on how to deal with competition. Many businesses face challenges that border on how to bring and keep customers to themselves. There are often many businesses that are competing for the same products or designs; they will all focus their attention on making the best version of the product that will suit the taste of the consumers. Often times, this leads to the availability of various versions of the same product in the market, and the consumers are now left with making their choices on which to go for. The ability of a business to focus, perceive rightly, and engage in adequate marketing will help the business record great success despite the competition.

Gaining Customer's loyalty

Following the challenge of the competition is the need to make sure that the customers you gain at first return to buy from you. This way, you have successfully converted a customer and gained his or her loyalty. To make your customers stay, you need a good marketing strategy. Social media, emails, and other communication mediums are essential tools you can rely on to overcome this challenge. The customers determine the future of a business. How you relate with your customers and treat them are some aspects of your business you need to pay attention to as well.

Uncertainty about the Future

The understanding that we do not know what the future holds is one other challenge that most businesses face. The world has more uncertainty today than it was in the past. This uncertainty can be seen as a result of global debt and economic struggles. However, when a business suffers from uncertainty, the business will not be able to have a long-term focus. Such businesses have no plans for the coming days. And when a business does not have plans for the future, a reduction in values is inevitable. You need to learn the art of balancing the need to have a short-term focus on the need for a long-term focus.

Stay away from uncertainty because it can deter you from achieving anything.

Change in Regulations

When your business is located in an environment that often experiences changes in its policies, the business is at risk of many challenges. Since you do not know what regulation might be made in the coming days, there will be a feeling of uncertainty, which will make it difficult for you to make certain decisions that will improve your business. The consideration for the environment has been among the major concern for most businesses. Usually, most businesses face challenges with regulations in the aspect of taxes and healthcare. There is still an argument on what the fiscal cliff is all about. On the part of the healthcare, the Affordable Health Care Act is complex that even both the state and local governments do not want to do, also, business owners need to give extra attention to it to have a full understanding of the law. The inability of businesses to decipher the plans of the government gives them a challenge with making certain decisions.

Solving Problems and Managing Risk

One area of challenge to many businesses is the ability to identify risks, assess them, and mitigate them. Many business owners lack the ability to solve problems, and this is telling on their abilities to deal with risks. As a result, many business managers are moving from one challenge to another setback. At times, the problems most of the businesses face are results of the changes occurring in the business environment. Hence, the right question one needs to ask is what problem requires solving? Every business needs to be well equipped to be able to solve problems. As you embark on your business, you need to have yourself trained on how to identify and deal with problems and risks.

Identifying the Right Staff

Many business owners have claimed that one of their greatest challenges has been getting the right and appropriate staff for their businesses. Being able to identify the best staff, get them to stay, and buy into the vision of the business is quite challenging. The truth is, there is no specific formula I can give you on how to get the best staff and make them stay. When your business is small, it is easier to monitor your staff and make them work effectively; this is because it is like a family at this stage. However, as your business grows, there will be an increase in the staffing challenge, with human resources becoming like politics. Every team member in any business has a lot of roles to play in the effectiveness of the business. Their personality and attitude toward work will have an impact on the productivity and harmony of the business. You need to learn how to deal with people and understand what often propels individuals to act in a certain way. Make it a conscious effort to identify the right set of people for your business, and you will be amazed at how much success you would record.

Aside from the challenges most businesses face, there are specific challenges that come with the 3D printing business. A report by Wohler's Associates claimed that the year 2020 will see to the increase in the market worth of the 3D printing to around US $21billion. This shows that the business is fast increasing and developing. Hence, the more challenges every investor needs to expect and prepare ahead to deal with. As an investor who will be considered a manufacturer, you need to be intimated about these challenges and know how to deal with them so as to have an impressive experience in your investment.

Lack of Standard

3D printing gives engineers and designers to make an object at a low price, and this often leads to a reduction in the quality of the product. Most 3D printers make objects with lower qualities when compared to the objects the traditional manufacturing techniques were used to make. Few of the 3D printers, including the High-end machines that are very expensive, are only able to make objects with good qualities. The reason for the low standard is the lack of a generally accepted standard. In other word, there is no general agreement on the possibility of having consistent durability, strength, and reliability on every object printed by the 3D printers between manufacturers and the consumers. Since there is no standard expected from the manufacturers, there are many substandard goods produced by these businesses. However, the American Makes and ANSI Additive Manufacturing Standardization Collaborative (AMSC) is making a move toward creating a harmonized standard and specifications for all businesses in the industry in order to deal with the challenge.

Impacts on the Environment

The commonest material that is used for most 3D printing works is plastic filament. The choice is based on the fact that it is not expensive. However, the byproducts gotten from it ends up in landfills. This is a move away from the environmental idea of doing away with reliance on plastic. There is the need to make use of the byproducts if there will be a widespread 3D printing in the industry. Also, another impact it has on the environment is its consumption of energy. According to a report at Loughborough University from research, 3D printers are said to make use of about 50 to 100 times more electrical energy compared to injection molding. More than all these, there has been a report that desktop 3D printer used for rapid prototyping and manufacturing in low volume t home and office releases nanosized particles that have the potentials to be harmful in indoor air. A way to deal with this is for exhaust ventilation or filtration accessories to come with 3D printers., and the printers need to be operated in a ventilated environment.

Expensive Equipment and Products

The equipment that you need to start a 3D printing business is quite expensive, and this has been an area of concern for most 3D professionals. Aside from the printers that make objects from plastic, which are quite cheap, other printers that require metals as materials are quite expensive, demanding up to thousands of dollars to procure. Also, to produce an object in a large volume is quite expensive, and it often takes longer to make items in large quantity, unlike the traditional manufacturing technique that supports large volume production.

Less Number of 3D printing Educated people

One area of challenge is the lack of general knowledge about 3D printing. There is what one can call a knowledge gap. Many employees do not have knowledge about it and how it works. They do not know the method of designing and its operation. Hence, you are likely to face a great challenge in this respect.

However, you can deal with it by training your employees on how to handle the 3D printer, and create designs. Nonetheless, this will demand your time and money, but if you are able to deal with, your business will experience tremendous bossing and growth.

There are Intellectual Property Complications

3D printing makes it easier to print a design anytime by anyone as long as there are a printer and the required material. As a result, the way people consider value has changed. Many people do not value the object itself, but most people now pay attention to the design. There is a need to address the intellectual property challenge. It is now easier for anyone to print another person's unprotected design that does not possess the quality that is intended or meet up with the measures of design. Such production can lead to insecurity for the public and would affect the designer leading to liability issues. For example, weapons are one way to look at it. There are many designs on guns that are quite available to the public. However, no one knows who will be held responsible if a person that is not legally permitted to hold a gun makes use of it.

Many manufacturers have faced these challenges, and for you as a startup, you are likely to come close to these challenges also. It, therefore, behooves you to take the necessary steps to deal with each of them to make your business grow successfully, and you can enjoy your investment. You may need to collaborate with other gurus in the industry and learn from them on how they have been able to deal with these challenges.

CHAPTER TEN

KNOW SOME COMMON PRODUCTS OF THE DEVICE

At this stage, I believe you have been equipped with all that you probably need to know about 3D printing and its business aspect. In this chapter, I will take you through some of the 3D printers you can lay your hands on in the market. These printers are great for commercial use and fit into any categories of user, either a hobbyist or the demand of an industry. Also, I selected the products based on affordability, ranging from the cheapest to the most expensive. The higher the capacity of the printer, the more expensive it is. With this chapter, you will have insight into the best printer you can go to kick start your 3D business. I am not listing these 3D printers in any specific order of importance. They all have their specific uses, which you will see soon. I have identified seven of the common and impressive 3D printers you may want to go for.

The MakerBot Replicator+

This printer is made as a successor to the MakerBot Replicator 3D printer, with newer developments to the previous Replicator. The development the Replicator+ has is in its speed and soundproof technology. It has a well-developed designing features as well as a great safety feature. However, it is an expensive printer costing US$1,899.99. It is designed to make use of polylactic acid (PLA) filament. It is a user-friendly machine that is designed for home use. The MakerBot Replicator+ uses the Fused Deposition Modeling as its print technology, and it weighs 22.8kg. It offers the following features:

Camera resolution: 640 x 480

Minimum layer resolution: 100 microns

Maximum layer resolution: 400 macrons

Dimensions: 528 x 441 x 410

The XYZprinting Da Vinci Mini

The Da Vinci Mini is a budget-friendly printer. It is among the cheapest means of getting into the 3D printing business. It costs US$248.88 and uses flakey software. It is easy to use and user-friendly at the same time. It is a compact printer, and that gives it its place in an office. It gives impressive printing despite its low price. The XYZprinting Da Vinci Mini utilizes the Fused Filament Fabrication as its print technology, and it has 10kg weight.

Minimum layer resolution: 100 microns

Maximum layer resolution: 400 macrons

Dimensions: 390 x 335 x 360mm

The Ultimaker 2+

This is the best professional 3D printer. It gives an awesome print quality, and this has earned it a place among professionals. For 3D modeling, the Ultimaker 2+ is a perfect option. It has an impressive and accurate 3D replications of ideas. However, the printer is expensive and does not work easily for beginners. It is also not suitable for home users since its primary purpose is to make professional models and prototypes. It has a very high resolution, basic interface, and open frame design. It cost US$2,999. The Ultimaker2+ makes use of the Fused Deposition Modeling as its print technology and weighs 11.3kg.

Minimum layer resolution: 20 microns

Maximum layer resolution: 600 macrons

Dimensions: 390 x 335 x 360mm

The FlashForge Creator Pro 2017

It is a mid-range 3D printer. It is not too expensive, not cheap. It stands in between. It is quite cheaper than pro models, and it gives quality products similar to what one would expect from a professional 3D printer. However, it is not as cheap as what a beginner would expect. It gives great accuracy in 3D model printing. The FlashForge is a noisy 3D printer and costs US$699. It depends on the Fused Deposition Modeling for its print technology.

Minimum layer resolution: 100 microns

Maximum layer resolution: 500 macrons

Dimensions: 526 x 360 x 389

The LulzBot Mini

It is a 3D printer for beginners. The LulzBot is very easy to operate, utilizes open-source hardware, slow, and make quite some noise. It is perfect for anyone learning 3D printing. With the open-source hardware, it is flexible and makes it easier for the community of makers to produce add-ons for the printer. It costs US$1,350 and relies on Fusion Deposition Modeling s its print technology, while it weighs 11,33kg.

Minimum layer resolution: 50 microns

Maximum layer resolution: 500 macrons

Dimensions: 435 x 340 x 385

The CubePro Trio

This 3D printer is a great three-colors and three materials printing. It gives good design and quite easy to use. Usually, home 3D printers give one or two color printing. However, the CubePro Trio defies the norm. It can print three materials in a single session. A good example of an instance when this printer can function is when you want to produce an enclosed mechanism. You can use nylon for the gears while you use ABS to surround and PLA to support the structure, which you can later dissolve using caustic soda. The printer is suitable for those who have an interest in modeling, and the professionals that are primarily interested in creating 3D objects that have moving parts. It is expensive to maintain but does not give impressive print quality. The CubePro Trio uses the Fused Deposition Modeling print technology, and it weighs 41kg.

Minimum layer resolution: 70 microns

Maximum layer resolution: 300 macrons

Dimensions: 578 x 591 x 578

The LulzBot Taz 6

It is a successor to the LulzBot Taz. Just like the Taz 5, the Taz 6 also has a solid open frame build, easy to use, and designed with a large print base. The Taz 6 is quite big and offers an impressive print quality. The print area is 280mm x 280mm x 250mm. It requires 2.85 filaments. The printer is very fast and gives wide support for materials. However, it is expensive and not totally reliable. The printer costsUS$3,037.65. And it weighs 19.5kg.

Minimum layer resolution: 75 microns

Maximum layer resolution: 300 macrons

Dimensions: 600 x 520 x 350.

CONCLUSION

You are welcome to the last part of this book. I hope it has been an awesome journey with me reading through the pages of this book. As I have said in the introductory part of this book, you would have arrived at a new horizon of knowledge at the end of this book. You don't have to join the league of those who wake up every morning to catch the taxi to complex headed by another person termed the "boss." If you have one, it is great; but if you do not have any, that should not be an end. It should rather be a means to an end. What I have offered you in this book is just the way to get to the end, which is to be on the path to *creating your wealth NOW*. I have shown you a way to make money through 3D printing. In the first part of this book, I took you through the use of 3D printing technology, also known as the additive manufacturing in certain industries. The purpose of that was to let you see its importance and the large market it has, so you can be assured that if you invest in it, you are not on your own. With this book, I believe you will achieve the Win you want. However, you may be feeling down and not wanting to take the right step. I tell you, there are three things you need to do to get started. They are:

Deal with your Mindset

I always tell people, to be successful, you need to deal with the playground of your thoughts – your mind. Having read this book, you may be afraid of losing your hard-earned money in a business you are just reading about for the first time. You may be thinking t is too stressful to engage in and time-consuming. Don't believe that thought is running into your head that it is too complex for you to do. Rather begin to see how much it is so possible to achieve, and you will be amazed at how well you would have successfully overcome your fear. Don't feel like you will manage what you have presently. Why not out your all into this and live beyond the scope of management. You were never created to manage. You only need to make use of the inner deposit of yours to make the right choices that will make you enjoy life as it is. Feed your mind with positive affirmations and tell yourself more about why you need to start planning toward the 3D printing business.

Follow the Right People

Once you are done reading this book, I expect you to look out for those who are knowledgeable about 3D printing, or who are already into the business and make them your friends. Learn from them. They will motivate you to take the necessary steps to become a 3D printing businessperson. Your relationship with them, aside from you getting motivated, will enhance your skills and experience about the business. You all will think in the same direction and share goals that have a similar basis. Hence, you would have freed yourself from anyone that may possibly try to talk you down.

Start Now!!!

I tell you, the best to have started the 3D business was right before you picked this book, while the second-best moment to start is right NOW. Avoid procrastination. If you need to acquire skills, enroll for it immediately, and start learning about it. Join the 3D Hubs platform and learn from their group and community. Make friends with designers, engineers, and professionals in the business already, and see for yourself the next step to take. Winning should not be postponed or procrastinated. You need to do it at the moment. It is you doing what is needed in the NOW. The time you have now is for you to implement the knowledge you have gained from this book. Never think of starting in the coming months or years. Such thoughts would deter you from making progress at it. It is either Now or never.

www.ingramcontent.com/pod-product-compliance
Lightning Source LLC
Chambersburg PA
CBHW070636220526
45466CB00001B/191